The BHS
Training Manual
FOR
Stage 1

D0932399

The BHS
Training Manual
FOR
Stage 1

THE BRITISH HORSE SOCIETY

Islay Auty FBHS

KENILWORTH PRESS

First published in 2003 by
Kenilworth Press

Reprinted 2005, 2006, 2007

British Library Cataloguing in Publication Data
A catalogue record for this book is available from the British Library

ISBN 978-1-872119-66-3

Layout by Kenilworth Press

Printed in Great Britain by Biddles, King's Lynn, Norfolk

KENILWORTH PRESS
An imprint of Quiller Publishing Ltd
Wykey House, Wykey, Shrewsbury, SY4 1JA
tel: 01939 261616 fax: 01939 261606
e-mail: info@quillerbooks.com
website: www.kenilworthpress.co.uk

Contents

Picture acknowledgements

All line drawings are by **Dianne Breeze**, with the exception of those on pages 38 (right), and 55, which are by **Carole Vincer**.

The arena diagrams on pages 86 and 87 are by **Michael J. Stevens**.

Picture sources
The author and publishers wish to acknowledge the following books as sources for some of the illustrations:

- **The BHS Manual of Equitation**, Consultant Editor Islay Auty FBHS, published by Kenilworth Press

- **The BHS Complete Manual of Stable Management,** Consultant Editor Islay Auty FBHS, published by Kenilworth Press

- **The BHS Instructors' Manual for Teaching Riding**, by Islay Auty FBHS, published by Kenilworth Press

- **Threshold Picture Guide No. 8, Field Management**, by Mary Gordon Watson, published by Kenilworth Press

- **Threshold Picture Guide No. 16, Feet and Shoes**, by Toni Webber, published by Kenilworth Press

- **The Horsemaster's Notebook**, by Mary Rose, published by Kenilworth Press

Introduction

What is the BHS Horse Knowledge and Riding Stage 1?

The four BHS Stage examinations, of which the Stage 1 is the first level, are generally taken by professional people wishing to work in the horse industry. The lower standards (primarily 1 and 2) are also used by keen amateur riders and horse owners who want to work for a valued qualification and achieve a standard of competence well recognised and respected in the horse industry. Each Stage exam includes a riding section, and a stable management section (called 'horse knowledge and care'). The two sections can be taken together on the same day, or separately. The complete qualification will not be awarded until both sections have been successfully achieved. Separate certificates are awarded for each section, and a final Stage 1 certificate.

The BHS Stage 1 Riding is a qualification which requires that the candidate is capable of riding a quiet, experienced horse or pony in an enclosed space, in walk, trot and canter. Candidates must understand the basic principles of horse care and working under supervision. They must show some knowledge and practice of looking after a well-mannered horse in the stable and at grass.

How is it accessed?

Training for the BHS Stage 1 exam is available at most BHS Approved riding schools throughout the UK, and certainly through every BHS 'Where to Train' centre. The British Horse Society runs a scheme of approval of riding schools and training centres whereby the establishments are regularly inspected on the quality and level of instruction they offer. Approved riding schools direct their teaching primarily at the leisure rider – those who ride weekly or more frequently for pleasure. Where to Train centres are specifically orientated towards trainees working towards a career in the horse industry, whether as full- or part-time employees. Most centres run some kind of structured training towards the Stage examinations. This training may be on a 'one day a week' basis, it might be in a weekly evening class, or it may be by private arrangement between the instructor and the individual concerned.

A qualified BHS instructor should be able to give you guidance as to your standard and ability and how much help and training you need towards your goal of taking and passing the BHS Stage 1 exam. The more highly qualified your instructor, and especially if he or she is a BHS examiner (which means they examine Stage 1 exams), the more able he/she should be to give you sound advice about how to train for and achieve the standard to which you aspire.

Training

It is impossible to say how much training is necessary because it will depend on:

- Your initial standard.

- How much time and effort you are able to commit to the goal of achieving Stage 1.

- How much financial commitment you are able to make to the training and the fees for sitting the exam.

- How you respond to training and therefore how quickly you progress.

- Other variables such as family commitments, unexpected circumstances, etc.

You should feel confident about the person with whom you will be training. It is important too, that you can work in a way that motivates you to further your own progress. There may be areas of the theory knowledge where you will need to study on your own. You may be able to work with other like-minded trainees, and this gives you the chance to gauge your progress against others working with the same aim. If you have a horse of your own at home you can practise the tasks that you will be expected to demonstrate in the exam.

How the Stage 1 is examined

All BHS examinations are taken at specially selected BHS examination centres. All exam centres have to be Where to Train centres and are guaranteed to offer a good standard of horses to ride and facilities in which to carry out the practical aspects of the exam. The exam is run by the BHS and a panel of examiners (three or four) under the organisation of a chief examiner. The chief examiner oversees the standard and guides the team who examine the competence of the candidates.

A Stage 1 exam usually takes approximately half a day to complete and the candidates (usually a maximum of eighteen in one day) are divided into three groups. Each candidate can expect to cover a large part of the syllabus in the work he or she is asked to demonstrate.

The syllabus is divided into **compulsory** and **supporting** elements. The compulsory elements are subjects that will certainly be examined and in which the candidate must demonstrate knowledge and competence. Supporting elements are less critical, **may** be examined and provide supporting evidence of competence.

Examiners are trained and experienced in both their ability to communicate well with you, the candidate, when you are nervous and apprehensive and to assess your overall competence at the level, in spite of nerves perhaps adversely affecting your performance. The examiners will:

- Aim to be friendly and 'human', putting you at ease.

- Be clear in all the questions they ask you and in their explanation of the tasks they require you to carry out.

- Be quick to rephrase a question if they think you are not clear about what they are looking for.

- Genuinely be looking to pass you on what you can do and do know, rather than trying to find fault and fail you.

- Genuinely be trying to help you to give your best, in spite of your inevitable nerves.

In return you must:

- Know your work thoroughly and have rehearsed or practised it until it is second nature to you and will come through even if you are a little nervous.

- Believe in yourself and in your ability to pass the exam.

- Acknowledge that you will feel nervous but do not allow your nerves to swamp you so that you are unable to demonstrate your competence.

Examiners never fail candidates who are up to standard, but candidates fail themselves if they allow their nerves to get the better of them.

- If you make a mistake, remember that while it may seem major to you it is probably fairly minor, and it will only be of consequence if you then allow the rest of your performance to be affected by your perception of that one mistake. You must be able to focus forward on the rest of your day even if you perceive that you have made a major error.

See also page 102 for further information on the exam day itself.

Note that you do need to be a member of the BHS to be able to apply to take a Stage exam.

Working with horses – a few words of advice

If you are embarking on a career in the horse industry and are taking this exam as the first rung on the ladder to professionally recognised qualifications, it will help to consider a few important points.

Your training should instil in you **high standards** which you should strive to adhere to. Take pride in working to a high standard and always produce work that is to the best of your ability.

Good manners, communication and **discipline** are essential in dealing with horses, which can be potentially dangerous if not managed in a well-disciplined 'safe' way. Personal discipline usually develops from a well-disciplined childhood, schooldays, or perhaps, in this case, in the training environment that you have now entered.

The nature of working with horses dictates that it is a very practical 'hands on' type of work, requiring that you develop and maintain **physical fitness**. When you first start working full-time with horses you may find the work very tiring, especially if you have been used to doing only your own horse(s) at home. You will come through this early period of fatigue and every day it will get better and easier. Make sure, though, that you pace yourself and do not end up physically exhausted. Avoid 'burning the candle at both ends', eat sensibly and leave time for one or two early nights a week, particularly if you have to get up early in the morning. Over the first three months your stamina and physical fitness will develop quite dramatically. From the start of your career with horses, make sure that you carry heavy weights correctly, balance yourself when you carry anything awkward, and use a sack trolley or similar to move bales or heavy items if you have no one to help you.

Stage 1
Horse Knowledge and Care

Syllabus

Candidates must be physically fit in order to carry out yard and fieldwork efficiently, without undue stress and strain. They will be expected to demonstrate competent use of time.

Candidates will be expected to give practical demonstrations, as well as be involved in discussion of selected tasks and topics.

> **IMPORTANT**: Candidates are advised to check that they are working from the latest examination syllabus, as examination content and procedure are liable to alteration. Contact the BHS Examinations Office for up-to-date information regarding the syllabus.

British Horse Society – Stage 1 Syllabus

Stage 1- Horse Knowledge and Care

Candidates must be physically fit in order to carry out yard and fieldwork efficiently without undue stress and strain. They will be expected to demonstrate competent use of time.
Candidates will be expected to give practical demonstrations as well as be involved in discussion of selected tasks and topics.

Unit code number S1CARE			
Learning Outcomes	**Element**	**Assessment criteria**	
The candidate should be able to:		The candidate has achieved this outcome because s/he can:	Influence
Grooming	1.1.1	Identify all items within the grooming kit	Supporting
	1.2.1	Give the uses and purpose of individual items within a grooming kit	Compulsory
Know how to;			
Groom a horse	1.3.1	Show the sequence of an effective grooming procedure when brushing off / quartering	Compulsory
Put on a tail bandage.			
	1.4.1	Give the reasons for grooming.	Supporting
	1.4.2	Apply safe procedures	Compulsory
	1.5.1	Show how to safely and efficiently apply a tail bandage	Compulsory
	1.5.2	Show how to safely and efficiently remove a tail bandage	Supporting
Clothing	2.1.1	Identify various stable rugs and their method of securing	Supporting
Know how to; Put on various	2.1.2	Identify Turn-out rugs and their methods of securing	Compulsory
types of rugs including a New Zealand.	2.2.1	Demonstrate the correct fitting of individual rugs and identify any faults	Supporting
Fit a roller, surcingle and cross surcingles and understand their	2.3.1	Demonstrate rugging-up appropriately with regard for safety	Compulsory
various uses. Take off horse clothing safely.	2.3.2	Demonstrate removing rugs appropriately with regard for safety	Compulsory
Saddlery	3.1.1	Identify the parts of the Saddle	Supporting
	3.1.2	Identify parts of the Bridle	Supporting
Know how to; Put on a saddle, a	3.1.3	Demonstrate how to put on a Martingale	Supporting
numnah and a snaffle bridle (with	3.1.4	Demonstrate how to put on a Hunting Breastplate	Supporting
appropriate noseband with	3.2.1	Recognise worn or damaged tack	Compulsory
martingale/ breastplate). Check	3.3.1	Discuss the consequences of worn or dirty tack	Supporting
tack for safety and comfort of	3.4.1	Demonstrate a safe and efficient method of tacking up	Compulsory
horse and rider. Remove tack and understand immediate	3.4.2	Demonstrate a safe and efficient method of un-tacking	Compulsory
aftercare. Recognise worn or ill-fitting saddlery, being aware of	3.5.1	Show how to fit a numnah	Compulsory
the dangers involved. Name	3.6.1	Show and or discuss how to secure various types of noseband	Compulsory
parts of the saddle and bridle.	3.7.1	Show and or discuss how to clean tack	Compulsory
Handling	4.1.1	Give the principles of safety when working with horses	Compulsory
Know how to; Put on, fit and care			
for headcollars, halters and lead	4.2.1	Show correct handling techniques	Compulsory
ropes. How and where to tie up a	4.3.1	Demonstrate how to put on a headcollar	Compulsory
horse, in the stable and outside.	4.4.1	Tie up horses safely and efficiently	Compulsory
Be practical and workmanlike.			
	4.5.1	Show efficient use of time in each task	Compulsory
	4.6.1	Maintain a clean working environment	Compulsory

STAGE 1 SYLLABUS JANUARY 2006

Stage 1 – Horse Knowledge and Care cont.

Unit code number S1CARE

Learning Outcomes	Element	Assessment criteria	Influence
The candidate should be able to:		The candidate has achieved this outcome because s/h_ can:	**Influence**
Horse husbandry	5.1.1	Give a variety of bedding materials	Supporting
	5.1.2	Give reasons for using different types of bedding	Supporting
Know; Types of Bedding. Mucking out. Bedding down. Skipping out. Setting fair. Building and maintaining a muck heap. Keeping all areas swept and tidy.	5.1.3	Show and or discuss how to maintain different types of bed	Supporting
	5.2.1	Demonstrate efficient, safe procedures for mucking out	Compulsory
	5.2.2	Demonstrate efficient, safe procedures for skipping out	Compulsory
	5.2.3	Demonstrate efficient, safe procedures for bedding down	Compulsory
	5.2.4	Demonstrate efficient, safe procedures for setting a bed fair	Compulsory
	5.3.1	Demonstrate safe efficient use of stable tools	Compulsory
	5.4.1	Describe how to build a muck heap	Supporting
Foot and Shoeing	6.1.1	Pick out feet into a skip	Compulsory
	6.1.2	Wash feet	Supporting
Know how to; Maintain the horses feet in good condition.	6.1.3	Oil hooves	Supporting
	6.2.1	Comment on the condition of the shoe in-front of you using correct terminology	Compulsory
Be able to; Recognise overgrown feet, risen clenches, worn, loose or 'sprung' shoes	6.3.1	Recognise a well shod foot	Compulsory
	6.3.2	Recognise long feet	Supporting
	6.3.3	Recognise risen clenches	Supporting
	6.3.4	Recognise worn shoes	Compulsory
Anatomy and Handling	7.1.1	Identify points of the horse	Compulsory
	7.2.1	Use correct terminology when describing the horses coat colour	Compulsory
Know; The main external areas (forehand, middle, hindquarters). Basic points of the horse, their colours and markings. How to stand a horse up correctly in the stable and/or outside. How to lead and turn horses at walk and trot. How to hold a reasonably quiet horse for treatment, shoeing and clipping.	7.2.2	Use correct terminology when describing horses markings	Compulsory
	7.3.1	Show how to hold a horse for treatment	Compulsory
	7.3.2	Show how to stand the horse up for inspection	Supporting
	7.4.1	Demonstrate safe, effective leading in hand at walk for an observer	Compulsory
	7.4.2	Demonstrate safe, effective leading in hand at trot for an observer	Supporting
	7.4.3	Demonstrate safe, correct turning of the horse when leading in hand for an observer	Compulsory
Health and Safety	8.1.1	Recognise hazardous lifting situations	Compulsory
Know; The importance of physical fitness in order to carry out yard work efficiently without stress and strain, use correct methods for stable tasks, lifting, moving heavy weights. How to fill, weigh and tie up a hay-net.	8.1.2	Show safe lifting procedures	Compulsory
	8.1.3	Show safe carrying procedures	Compulsory
	8.2.1	Show how to fill a haynet	Supporting
	8.2.2	Show how to weigh a haynet	Supporting
	8.2.3	Show how to safely and efficiently tie up a haynet	Compulsory
	8.2.4	Recognise potential dangers when using a haynet	Supporting
Horse Health	9.1.1	State what you must look for at Morning inspections	Supporting
Know the signs of good health in horses and ponies recognise when they are off-colour and the importance of an immediate report.	9.1.2	State what you must look for at last thing at night inspections	Supporting
	9.2.1	Recognise signs of good health	Compulsory
	9.2.2	Recognise signs of ill health	Compulsory
	9.3.1	Give the reasons for reporting when a horse is unwell	Compulsory

Stage 1 – Horse Knowledge and Care cont.

Unit code number S1CARE			
Learning Outcomes	**Element**	**Assessment criteria**	
The candidate should be able to:		The candidate has achieved this outcome because s/he can:	**Influence**
Horse Behaviour	10.1.1	Outline the horses lifestyle in the wild	Supporting
	10.2.1	Describe the horses basic instincts of survival	Supporting
	10.3.1	Describe how to handle the horse in the stable	Compulsory
Show knowledge of the horse's natural life-style, instincts, actions and reactions.	10.3.2	Describe how to handle the horse in the field	Compulsory
	10.3.3	Describe how to handle the horse when ridden	Compulsory
	10.4.1	Describe signs of danger as shown in the horses expression when in the field	Supporting
	10.4.2	Describe signs of danger as shown in the horses expression when in the stable	Supporting
	10.4.3	Describe signs of danger as shown in the horses expression when ridden	Supporting
Basic Grassland Care	11.1.1	Describe a "horse-sick" field	Supporting
	11.1.2	Give ways a horse sick field can be avoided/ remedied	Supporting
Know; What to look for in and around the field. Daily inspections. How to turn out a horse, how to catch him and bring him in from the field. Recognise a horse sick field.	11.2.1	Describe what to check each day in the field	Compulsory
	11.3.1	Describe acceptable, safe methods of turning a horse out into a field	Compulsory
	11.3.2	Describe acceptable, safe methods of bringing a horse in from a field	Compulsory
Watering & Feeding	12.1.1	Name, Oats, Barley, Sugarbeet, Bran, Coarse mix, Nuts/Cubes, Chaff.	Compulsory
	12.1.2	Recognise good quality, Oats, Barley, Sugarbeet pulp/ cubes, Bran, Coarse mix, Nuts/Cubes, Chaff.	Supporting
Know; General principles and the importance of cleanliness. The various types of fodder in general use, and recognise good and bad quality. Suitable feeding of horses and ponies in light work.	12.1.3	Recognise poor quality, Oats, Barley, Sugarbeet pulp/ cubes, Bran, Coarse mix, Nuts/Cubes, Chaff.	Supporting
	12.2.1	Recognise good quality hay	Supporting
	12.2.2	Recognise bad quality hay	Supporting
	12.2.3	Recognise acceptable quality hay	Supporting
	12.3.1	Recognise good quality haylage	Supporting
	12.3.2	Recognise bad quality haylage	Supporting
Definition of 'light work'; Daily walk trot canter where the horse is not stressed.	12.4.1	Discuss the dangers of feeding poor quality fodder	Supporting
	12.5.1	Give the rules of good feeding	Compulsory
	12.6.1	Give the rules of watering	Compulsory
	12.6.2	Know the importance of cleanliness	Supporting
	12.7.1	Discuss suitable feed for a grass kept horse and or pony in light work throughout the seasons	Compulsory
	12.7.2	Discuss suitable daily quantity of feed for a grass kept horse and or pony in light work throughout the seasons	Supporting
	12.8.1	Discuss suitable feed for a stabled horse and or pony in light work	Compulsory
	12.8.2	Discuss suitable daily quantity of feed for a stabled horse and or in light work	Supporting
	12.9.1	Discuss suitable methods of watering horses, at grass	Compulsory
	12.9.2	Discuss suitable methods of feeding horses, at grass	Supporting
General Knowledge Know the risks and responsibilities involved when riding or leading on the public highway. Know the correct procedures in the event of an accident. Safety Rules and Fire Precautions. Knowledge of the British Horse Society's aims	13.1.1	Describe suitable clothes to wear when working with horses	Compulsory
	13.2.1	Describe fire precautions in the work place	Compulsory
	13.3.1	Give the correct procedure in the event of an accident to a person	Compulsory
	13.4.1	Give the safety rules for riding in a class	Supporting
	13.4.2	Give the rules and good manners involved when taking horses on the public highway	Compulsory
	13.5.1	Give the aims of the British Horse Society.	Supporting

As you can see from the syllabus, the knowledge and practical ability that you require for the Stage 1 exam is very clearly disseminated into 'elements'. This is to encourage you to be systematic in your training and to ensure that your practical ability is underpinned with the necessary background knowledge.

Do not be anxious that every single 'element' as listed will be examined, or that you will fail if you do not know an answer in one specific subject. As with any examination, the syllabus requires extensive study while the examination will test a section of the overall knowledge. You can be sure, though, that the examiner will want to see that your competence in handling horses in various situations at this level is supported by sound knowledge.

Notice, too, that the syllabus contains 'compulsory' and 'supporting' elements. Compulsory elements can appear in both the practical and theory sections of your exam. The supporting elements, as the name suggests, add weight to the demonstration of competence that the compulsory elements should show. During your training and studying, remember to check regularly which areas of each subject are compulsory and which are supporting. Make quite sure that you are competent and confident about **all** the compulsory elements. Make sure that you are familiar with all the supporting elements – there should be nothing within the syllabus that you have never heard of!

The following sections show the learning outcomes, elements and assessment criteria, in line with the syllabus; for ease of studying, the subjects will be listed under the element number followed by 'what the examiner will look for'.

NOTE

The following symbols are used throughout this book
when referring to elements of the syllabus:

C   COMPULSORY

S   SUPPORTING

Grooming

Groom a horse.

Put on a tail bandage.

ELEMENT

S	**1.1.1**	Identify all items within the grooming kit.
C	**1.2.1**	Give the uses and purpose of individual items within a grooming kit.
C	**1.3.1**	Show the sequence of an effective grooming procedure when brushing off/quartering.
S	**1.4.1**	Give the reasons for grooming.
C	**1.4.2**	Apply safe procedures.
C	**1.5.1**	Show how to safely and efficiently apply a tail bandage.
S	**1.5.2**	Show how to safely and efficiently remove a tail bandage.

What the examiner is looking for

- You are likely to be asked to carry out a grooming procedure with a stabled horse. (Element 1.3.1)

- Within this procedure you will probably be asked which item of grooming kit you are using and what is the purpose of each item. (Element 1.2.1)

- You should understand the difference between quartering the horse (prior to exercise), brushing the horse off (grooming to clean up the horse after work), and a full grooming sequence (the main groom of the day, perhaps soon after exercise). (Element 1.3.1)

- You may be asked to discuss the difference between grooming a grass-kept horse and a stabled horse.

- You should be able to demonstrate competent and effective grooming of a stabled horse. You may be asked to pick out the horse's feet, use a dandy brush, and groom using a body brush and curry comb.

- You may be asked to show how to groom a mane or tail. Be clear about managing the tail and that often it is preferable only to finger through the tail to prevent damage to long tail hairs by excessive brushing.

- Be able to groom the horse's head carefully but effectively.

- Understand the need to clean and know how to deal with the eyes, mouth, nose, dock and sheath.

- You are likely to be asked why grooming is necessary, and you should be able to give health, cleanliness, comfort, safety, improving well-being and fitness among your answers. (Element 1.4.1)

- You must demonstrate safe procedures at all times. These should include awareness of the horse and how the horse is reacting to you. The horse should be

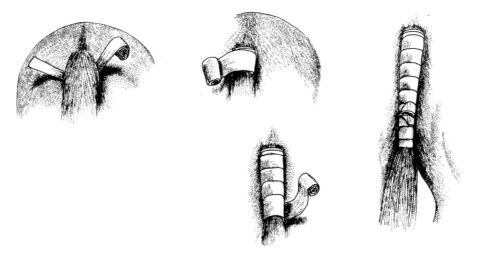

Putting on a tail bandage.

safely tied up on most occasions when you are dealing with him. If the horse is not tied up but you are in the stable, then the door should be shut. Equipment should be kept tidy and organised. Always be in a safe position in relation to the position of the horse (e.g. not close to a wall when picking up hind feet).

- You will be asked to apply a tail bandage. You should be able to discuss when such a bandage might be used, how long it would be used for and how to remove it. (Elements 1.5.1 and 1.5.2) Remember: if removing a tail bandage from a horse with a plaited tail then the bandage must be unrolled and cannot be pulled off.

Take every opportunity to groom as many different horses as you can, both stabled and at grass. When asked to demonstrate grooming, set about the task with a purpose, as if you really want the horse's coat to gleam. Grooming is a good experience for anyone who cares about horses and most horses thoroughly enjoy the process. For Stage 1 you must show a quiet confidence in handling well-behaved horses, and a practical ability to groom a horse effectively and apply a tail bandage.

Clothing

Put on various types of rugs including a New Zealand.

Fit a roller, surcingle and cross surcingles and understand their various uses.

Take off horse clothing safely.

ELEMENT

S	**2.1.1**	Identify various stable rugs and their methods of securing.
C	**2.1.2**	Identify turn-out rugs and their methods of securing.
S	**2.2.1**	Demonstrate the correct fitting of individual rugs and identify any faults.
C	**2.3.1**	Demonstrate rugging-up appropriately with regard for safety.
C	**2.3.2**	Demonstrate removing rugs appropriately with regard for safety.

What the examiner is looking for

- You will be asked to apply rugs to a stabled horse. (Elements 2.3.1 and 2.3.2)

- The type of rug you are asked to apply may depend on the time of year and the weather conditions. You may need to make a choice of rug – say, a summer sheet for a warm, sunny day or a heavier stable rug for a colder winter's day.

- You should be familiar with the range of rugs which may be used through the year for stabled horses. Be aware of the difference in the way rugs are attached, either with more old-fashioned rollers or surcingles, or with more modern cross-surcingle attachments. (Element 2.1.1)

- You are likely to be asked to fit a New Zealand rug. New Zealand rugs are traditionally used for turn-out but there is a wide range of turn-out rugs available today. Turn-out rugs vary in weight and have various means of attachment. Make sure that you have tried to see several different ways in which rugs are fitted and attached. (Element 2.1.2)

- It is likely that you will have to discuss correct rug fittting. You must show that you understand how a rug should fit around the neck, along the back (correct length) and down the body (correct depth); you should also know about the overall suitability of attachments for securing the rug safely in place.

- Throughout your application and removal of rugs, you must demonstrate safety in your handling of the horse and safe positioning of yourself in relation to the horse. Awareness is the key word. (Elements 2.3.1 and 2.3.2)

- In most cases it is safer to fold a rug when applying it to a horse that you do not know. Make sure you are entirely familiar with and competent about applying folded rugs over the wither, as opposed to throwing rugs onto the horse.

- Whilst it would be usual to remove several rugs or blankets together, be sure that all attachments have been undone so that the rugs can all be smoothly slid off the horse's hindquarters.

Horse clothing designs change nearly every year, and each type of rug updates the last for lightness, warmth, waterproof properties, etc. Your role is to try to identify the rugs you are asked to fit and describe them to the best of your ability in terms of how they fit the horse and what their role is.

Stable rugs come in various weights according to summer or winter use. Mostly they are attached by cross-surcingles, which fit under the horse's belly, crossing underneath. Some rugs are still attached with an old-fashioned single roller around the girth region, and are often fitted with some type of pad over the horse's back.

New Zealand rugs, which are broadly recognised as any rug which is used for outdoor purposes and has waterproof properties, are attached by a variety of methods; you must check the rug carefully to see where the straps and attachments are applied.

If considering the general application of rugs then the following guidelines should help:

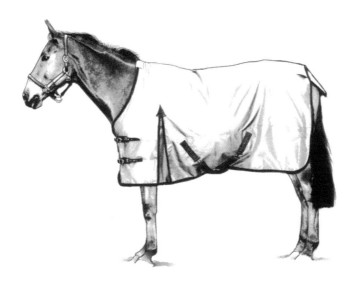

A well-fitted New Zealand rug, with gussets at the shoulder to allow for room and flexibility of movement

- First, decide what type of rug it is and which purpose it will serve. For example, is it waterproof? Nylon quilted? Lightweight? Anti-sweat? Or a fleece-type under-rug?

- Check what straps it has, and if it has hind-leg straps clip them up out of the way so that they do not flap as you apply the rug.

- Have the horse tied up.

- Fold the rug in half so that it is easy to place over the horse's withers, and then unfold it once roughly in place.

- Attach the front buckle and slide the rug into place without pulling it too far back.

- Attach the cross-surcingles, back-leg straps, or a pad and roller as appropriate.

- Check the overall fit of the rug to ensure that the horse is safe and comfortable.

A rug fits if:

- There is room around the neck and the shoulders are well covered.

APPLYING A RUG.

A folded rug, placed well up over the withers, is being secured in front.

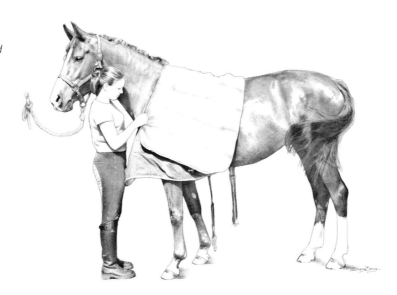

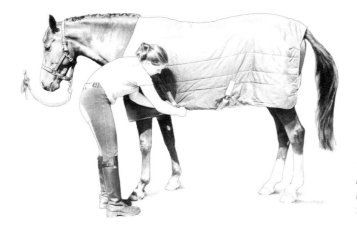

With the rug unfolded and in place, the attachments – here cross-surcingles – are fastened.

- The rug is deep enough to come down at least to just below the elbow (much deeper with some outdoor rugs).

- The rug is long enough to come almost to the root of the tail; some rugs have an extended area over the horse's dock (particularly outdoor rugs).

- The straps are adjusted to be snug but not tight, not loose and sagging so the horse could get caught in them.

You must demonstrate competence in handling rugs, putting them on and removing them efficiently, without inconveniencing the horse in any way.

Either place the rugs over the stable door as you remove them (if the stable is indoors or has an overhang over it) or remove them at once to a suitable storage area. Don't leave rugs on the stable floor where they can pick up bedding or get damp, or where some horses may chew them.

Saddlery

Know how to:

Put on a saddle, a numnah, a snaffle bridle (with appropriate noseband with martingale/breastplate).

Check tack for safety and comfort of horse and rider.

Remove tack and understand immediate aftercare.

Recognise worn or ill-fitting saddlery, being aware of the dangers involved.

Name parts of the saddle and bridle.

ELEMENT

S	**3.1.1** Identify the parts of the saddle.
S	**3.1.2** Identify the parts of the bridle.
S	**3.1.3** Demonstrate how to put on a martingale.
S	**3.1.4** Demonstrate how to put on a hunting breastplate.
C	**3.2.1** Recognise worn or damaged tack.
S	**3.3.1** Discuss the consequences of worn or dirty tack.
C	**3.4.1** Demonstrate a safe and efficient method of tacking up.
C	**3.4.2** Demonstrate a safe and efficient method of untacking.
C	**3.5.1** Show how to fit a numnah.
C	**3.6.1** Show and/or discuss how to secure various types of noseband.
C	**3.7.1** Show and/or discuss how to clean tack.

What the examiner is looking for

- You will be asked to put on a snaffle bridle and saddle and then remove them again. Your procedure for doing this should demonstrate safety and awareness of the horse and yourself. (Elements 3.4.1. and 3.4.2)

- The tack should belong to the horse, in which case it should fit him. However, you should be capable of recognising that the overall appearance of the fit is comfortable and looks correct for the horse.

- Be able to consider the overall appearance of the bridle. When discussing the bridle with the examiner make sure that you have removed the headcollar if the horse was tied up before the examiner arrived. It is impossible to clearly discuss a bridle if there is a headcollar over it.

- You will probably be asked to name the parts of the saddle and bridle. (Elements 3.1.1.and 3.1.2)

- You should be able to recognise the condition of supple, well-maintained tack, and to describe tack that is neglected, cracking and dry even if the latter is not in front of you. (Element 3.2.1)

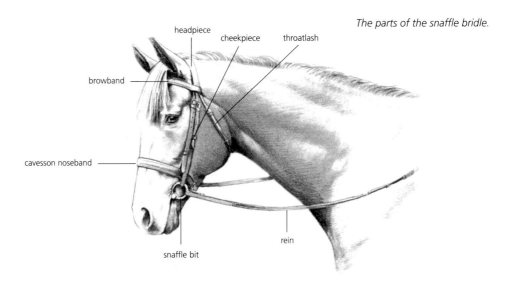

The parts of the snaffle bridle.

headpiece

cheekpiece

throatlash

browband

cavesson noseband

rein

snaffle bit

The parts of the saddle.

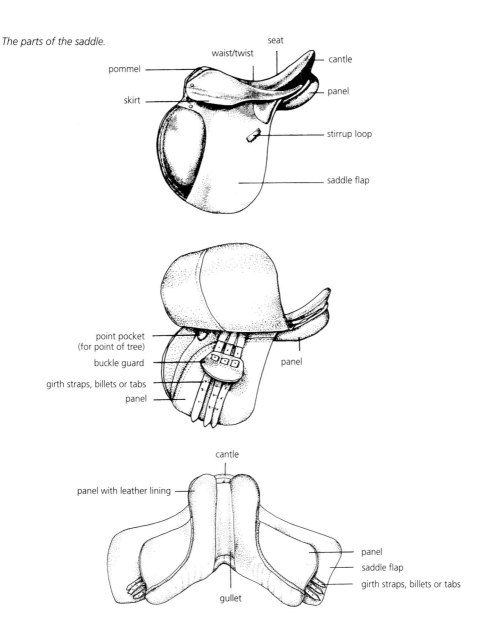

- Be able to talk about the danger and discomfort to horse and rider of using tack that is in poor condition or repair. (Element 3.3.1)

- Your application of the saddle is likely to include the use of a numnah. (Element 3.5.1) Try to familiarise yourself with different types of numnah and ensure that you can attach them to the saddle or girth to keep them in place in use. Ensure that the numnah fits well under the saddle and allows freedom over the wither.

- You will be asked to put on a hunting breastplate and/or a martingale. (Elements 3.1.3 and 3.1.4) The martingale will usually be a 'running' type, and you should check that there are 'stops' on the reins for safety. Be aware of why these pieces of equipment are used and make sure you have practised well with both.

- You may be asked to describe various different types of noseband and how these differ in the way they are applied to the horse. (Element 3.6.1) The bridle will carry one type of noseband and this will be discussed when you apply the bridle. Different nosebands may be on display for you to handle and identify.

- You may be asked to demonstrate how to clean tack, but it is more likely that you will be questioned on the method for cleaning tack. You may be asked how frequently you would clean tack and what to do with it if it was wet or muddy. (Element 3.7.1)

Your handling of the horse should demonstrate confidence and show familiarity with tacking up. You must also be able to complete the tasks in a reasonable timescale.

Handling

Know how to:

Put on, fit and care for headcollars, halters and lead ropes.

How and where to tie up a horse, in the stable and outside.

Be practical and workmanlike.

ELEMENT

- C **4.1.1** Give the principles of safety when working with horses.

- C **4.2.1** Show correct handling techniques.

- C **4.3.1** Demonstrate how to put on a headcollar.

- C **4.4.1** Tie up horses safely and efficiently.

- C **4.5.1** Show efficient use of time in each task.

- C **4.6.1** Maintain a clean working environment.

What the examiner is looking for

- **Always** awareness – awareness of how the horse is interacting with you around him, and awareness of your actions in relation to him. (Element 4.1.1) This element will cover your overall confidence and competence and relates to your whole manner throughout the practical part of the exam. (Element 4.2.1)

- You must show quiet confidence in your approach to any horse (horses you may not know or have handled before)

- Be able to place the headcollar on the horse and secure it firmly. (Element 4.3.1)

- Tie the horse up with a quick-release knot (see page 32). Preferably tie the rope through a thin piece of binder twine and not directly to the ring. If there is no twine on the ring then ask for some and state your reason for being unhappy to

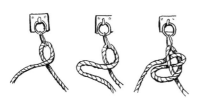

How to tie a quick-release knot.

tie the horse directly to the ring – i.e. in case the horse pulled back and injured himself. (Element 4.4.1)

- You may be asked to discuss where it is safe to tie up horses. In stables it would usually be considered safe to leave a horse tied up in his own stable with the door shut. If the horse is tied outside then other considerations might be taken into account: e.g. the weather, or outside distractions such as other horses, noises or frightening disturbances. It would be a sensible precaution not to leave an unsupervised horse tied up outside.

- Safe handling involves competence and awareness – both of which should be demonstrated in your exam.

- With competence and confidence come economy in time used for tasks. As you become more proficient, all your tasks will take you less time and you therefore develop efficiency.

- Work efficiently and tidily. Pick up droppings from the stable before you start any practical work and if a horse passes droppings while you are working then remove the dung. (Element 4.6.1.)

- Keep the yard area in which you are working swept and tidy. if you are working with other students you should all be reponsible for 'your own patch'. In this way the whole yard will stay smart and presentable at all times.

- Make sure that you are aware of things like dirty water buckets (straw or shavings in the water), droppings in the bed, muck heap becoming untidy, and take responsibility for maintaining every part of your working environment as neatly and cleanly as you can. This not only helps the professional appearance of a yard but also ensures that the horses' health is safeguarded through good stable management.

Horse Husbandry

Know:

Types of bedding.

Mucking out.

Bedding down.

Skipping out.

Setting fair.

Building and maintaining a muck heap.

Keeping all areas swept and tidy.

ELEMENT

| S | **5.1.1** | Give a variety of bedding materials. |

S **5.1.1** Give a variety of bedding materials.

S **5.1.2** Give reasons for using different types of bedding.

S **5.1.3** Show and/or discuss how to maintain different types of bed.

C **5.2.1** Demonstrate efficient, safe procedures for mucking out.

C **5.2.2** Demonstrate efficient, safe procedures for skipping out.

C **5.2.3** Demonstrate efficient, safe procedures for bedding down.

C **5.2.4** Demonstrate efficient, safe procedures for setting a bed fair.

C **5.3.1** Demonstrate safe, efficient use of stable tools.

S **5.4.1** Describe how to build a muck heap.

What the examiner is looking for

- You should be familiar with most common forms of bedding, e.g. straw, shavings, paper, sawdust, rubber matting (with a reduced amount of some other bedding). (Element 5.1.1)

- You should be able to discuss why different types of bedding are used. This may be due to availability, cost, ease of disposal, personal choice or commodity that is best for a particular horse. (Element 5.1.2)

- You will be expected to discuss how to maintain some of the bedding types you have named. You should be familiar with what you use 'at home', and in addition try to be competent with at least one other type of bedding.

- You may be asked to muck out a complete stable, or you may be involved in this as a group task. In every case the procedure for organising the task and then completing it is of importance. (Element 5.2.1)

- You may be asked to bed down a stable. (Element 5.2.3)

- Be able to demonstrate the difference between mucking out the box and skipping out (removal of droppings and tidying the bed). Be clear about how to set the bed fair. You may be asked to show this. (Elements 5.2.2 and 5.2.4)

- You should demonstrate competence in handling tools for use in the stable yard including awareness of safe management and storage of tools. (Element 5.3.1)

- You may be asked how to build a muck heap, or you may be taken to look at the exam centre's muck heap and asked to comment on it. You should be conversant with the tidy building and maintenance of a muck heap and its relevance to good yard management. (Element 5.4.1)

As a member of a team in a stable yard, everyone has joint responsibility for keeping tools and equipment safely stored and managed while in use. Wheelbarrows and forks can be dangerous to horses and humans in the wrong circumstances. A tidy, well-kept yard reflects the efficiency of those who work in the establishment.

Foot and Shoeing

Know how to:

Maintain the horse's feet in good condition.

Be able to recognise overgrown feet, risen clenches, worn, loose or 'sprung' shoes.

C **6.1.1** Pick out feet into a skip.

S **6.1.2** Wash feet.

S **6.1.3** Oil hooves.

C **6.2.1** Comment on the shoe in front of you, using correct terminology.

C **6.3.1** Recognise a well-shod foot.

S **6.3.2** Recognise long feet.

S **6.3.3** Recognise risen clenches.

C **6.3.4** Recognise worn shoes.

What the examiner is looking for

You should already be aware that care of the horse's feet on a daily basis is one of the most essential areas of good horse management. The old saying, 'no foot, no horse' is a very relevant statement, which has perpetuated through generations because of its truth.

Care of the horse's feet should be an integral part of the daily care and management of the horse but particularly those which are stabled for much of their time.

How to pick up a near fore.

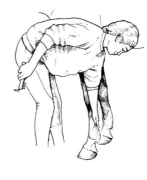

How to pick up a near hind.

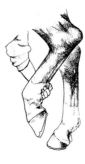

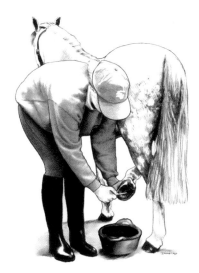

Horses become familiar with having all four feet picked up from the near side. Safe handling of the off hind from the near side.

Through regular and daily practice you must be able to:

- Pick out the horse's feet using a skip under each foot in turn to catch the dirt. (Element 6.1.1)

- You must demonstrate safe procedure for picking up the feet – particularly the hind feet, which should be held in such a way that you are not at risk from the horse unexpectedly kicking back.

- Picking up all four feet from the same side, if the horse is familiar with this practice, is labour and time-saving. However, a young or unbalanced horse may require that you move around from one side to the other to pick out the feet efficiently.

- Demonstrate an awareness and competence of when to pick up all four feet from the nearside and when to move around the horse.

- Management of the skip and the hoof pick is also relevant to the overall safety and procedure for carrying out the task competently.

- You may be asked to discuss when you would wash the horse's feet, and this would include such times as returning from a muddy hack or competition or when bringing the horse in from the field. (Element 6.1.2)

- You should understand that drying the horse's heels well after washing the feet is important to prevent possible chafing or 'cracking'.

■ It may be appropriate to grease the heels of a horse who is sensitive or prone to soreness, prior to washing the feet.

■ When washing feet care must be taken that the horse is familiar with the process and not frightened by a running hose or bucket of water sloshing in his vicinity.

■ You should show an ability to oil the hooves with efficiency and safety. (Element 6.1.3) The feet should be oiled thoroughly all over the outer wall, up into the coronary band and on the soles of the feet, covering the heels and the frog. Understand the value of the use of hoof oil in maintaining the suppleness of the horn as well as giving a polished appearance to the horse.

■ When commenting on the condition of a foot in front of you, look systematically for the following features (Elements 6.2.1, 6.3.1–6.3.4):

1. The snugness of the shoe to the foot; the shoe looking secure on the foot; and there being no visible signs of the clenches (nails on the outside wall of the foot) rising up and away from the wall.

2. All the clenches should be smooth, flush to the wall of the hoof and in a neat line about a third of the way up the wall from the floor.

3. The foot should not appear to be overgrowing the shoe in any area.

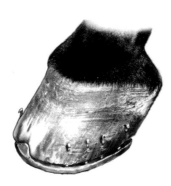

A foot in need of reshoeing – long toe, risen clenches, the shoe appears loose, and the heel is no longer supported by the shoe.

A good, well-shod foot – the shoe fits snugly, the clenches (nails) are flush with the hoof wall, and the heel of the shoe is long, offering good support to the horn at the heel.

4. The shoe should look sturdy and have no worn parts.

5. The groove in the shoe should be visible, with the nail heads well bedded down into the groove.

6. Toe or quarter clips, if present, should be flush with the wall and not dented into the foot itself.

7. The heels of the shoe should proceed well out in the heel region of the foot and not appear to finish short of the end of the frog.

- Long feet (Element 6.3.2) will look as if the toe of the foot extends forward; viewed from the side, the weight of the horse will appear to be concentrated in the heel region of the foot. The hoof/pastern axis will appear to be broken backwards.

Anatomy and Handling

Know:

The main external areas (forehand, middle, hindquarters).

Basic points of the horse, colours and markings.

How to stand a horse up correctly in the stable and/or outside.

How to lead and turn horses at walk and trot.

How to hold a reasonably quiet horse for treatment, shoeing and clipping.

ELEMENT

| C | **7.1.1** | Identify points of the horse. |

C **7.1.1** Identify points of the horse.

C **7.2.1** Use correct terminology when describing the horse's coat colour.

C **7.2.2** Use correct terminology when describing horse's markings.

C **7.3.1** Show how to hold a horse for treatment.

S **7.3.2** Show how to stand a horse up for inspection.

C **7.4.1** Demonstrate safe, effective leading in hand at walk for an observer.

S **7.4.2** Demonstrate safe, effective leading in hand at trot for an observer.

C **7.4.3** Demonstrate safe, correct turning of the horse when leading in hand for an observer.

What the examiner is looking for

- You should try to learn as many different colours of horses as possible and be familiar with how to identify the basic markings found on horses and how these

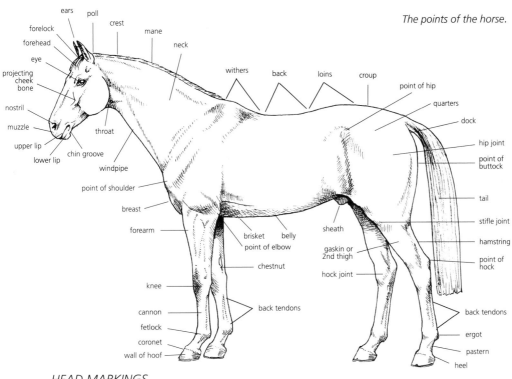

The points of the horse.

ears
poll
crest
mane
forelock
forehead
neck
eye
withers
back
loins
croup
projecting cheek bone
point of hip
nostril
quarters
muzzle
dock
upper lip
throat
hip joint
lower lip
chin groove
point of buttock
windpipe
point of shoulder
tail
breast
stifle joint
forearm
sheath
hamstring
brisket
belly
gaskin or 2nd thigh
point of hock
point of elbow
chestnut
hock joint
knee
cannon
back tendons
back tendons
fetlock
ergot
coronet
pastern
wall of hoof
heel

HEAD MARKINGS

Star.

Star and stripe.

Snip.

Blaze, extending to both nostrils.

White face.

MUZZLE MARKINGS

Snip and lip marks.

White upper and lower lips.

White muzzle.

Sock (left) and stocking markings.

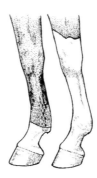

are correctly described. This will require some book work, and then you must try and look at as many different horses as you can 'in the flesh'. If you go to a competition you could practise by looking at a horse's colours and markings and imagine describing that horse to someone who hasn't seen him. You must also learn the basic points of the horse and be able to identify these on a live horse. (Elements 7.1.1, 7.2.1 and 7.2.2)

- You will be asked to show how to hold a horse for treatment. (Element 7.3.1) It would usually be sensible to keep the horse in the stable where the confinement of the four walls may help your control. The priority for holding a horse for treatment is that you should be on the same side of the horse as the person treating the horse. If the horse throws himself about you are both able to move

How to stand a horse up for inspection.

out of the way on the same side. If necessary, put the horse's bottom into a corner and keep him close to one of the stable walls where you can gain more control of him.

- You may be asked to hold up a front leg to help restrain the horse. In this case, stand near to the foreleg and pick up the leg, bending the knee; support the limb along the cannon bone, and stand facing the horse's tail, holding the leg on the same side as the area being treated. Always give the other person a few seconds' warning if you feel you will have to let go of the leg. Try to keep your eyes on the person treating the horse, so that you are aware of what they are doing.

- If asked to stand a horse up for inspection (Element 7.3.2), it would be more appropriate to bring the horse out onto the yard (as if for a vet or potential purchaser to observe). If in doubt, put a bridle on the horse. Only bring the horse out in a headcollar if you are advised that it is safe to do so. If the decision is left to you, with a horse you do not know, always choose the safe option and use a bridle. Stand the horse in the yard on as level a surface as possible. Try to make the horse stand square, taking weight on all four feet. Either stand in front of the horse with one hand on either side of the bridle, one rein in each hand facing the horse (you are then not in the observer's view), or stand close to the horse's head on the left hand side if he is fractious and likely to jump forward.

- Leading the horse in hand (Elements 7.4.1–7.4.3) whether in walk or trot requires

The correct way to lead a horse/pony.

How not to lead a horse/pony. Handler too far in advance – control could not be maintained.

you to be firmly in control and to produce a lively forward-going walk or trot on a good straight line.

- When leading, always turn the horse away from you. This enables you to keep control of the hindquarters and prevent them swinging around; it also reduces the likelihood of the horse treading on you. Learn to use your voice to communicate with the horse: calm him if he is a bit full of himself and encourage him if he is lazy. With a really lazy horse it is useful to learn how to use a short whip to encourage him into more active participation.

When turning, turn the horse away from you.

- If trotting the horse in hand, you should start smoothly in walk, progress into trot, return smoothly to walk before turning, and then ease back into trot, being aware that the horse may be more forward-thinking on the return. Always make the turn in walk.

Health and Safety

The importance of physical fitness in order to carry out yard work efficiently without stress and strain.

Use correct methods for stable tasks, lifting, moving heavy weights.

How to fill, weigh and tie up a haynet.

ELEMENT

C	**8.1.1** Recognise hazardous lifting situations.
C	**8.1.2** Show safe lifting procedures.
C	**8.1.3** Show safe carrying procedures.
S	**8.2.1** Show how to fill a haynet.
S	**8.2.2** Show how to weigh a haynet.
C	**8.2.3** Show how to safely and efficiently tie up a haynet.
S	**8.2.4** Recognise potential dangers when using a haynet.

What the examiner is looking for

- You should be aware that when working with horses there will be instances where your own safety and welfare is compromised if you do not carry out safe procedures when moving and lifting heavy materials.

- Lifting bales, feed sacks and full water buckets are all instances where correct lifting methods are important. (Element 8.1.1)

- When picking up a heavy weight (such as a feed sack), always bend your knees and keep your back in the vertical plane. Either take the weight of the object across your chest or put the weight onto your shoulder(s).

- When picking up full buckets of water, keep the knees bent and ideally balance one bucket by having an equal weight (another bucket) in the other hand.

- Carry bales of hay and straw in a twosome with a second person.

How to pick up two buckets correctly.

How to pick up a feed sack – knees bent, back straight, with the weight supported on the torso.

Sharing the weight of a bale, with one person on either side.

Knees bent and back straight, to individually move a bale.

- If asked to fill a haynet, it is usual to shake the hay slightly (not extensively so that seed is lost) so that it is easier to stuff into the open neck of the net. (Element 8.2.1) Fill the haynet as required: small haynets may weigh 1.8kg/4lb whereas a net to last a horse overnight may hold 4.5–6.5kg/10–14lb. Close the neck by pulling the drawstring tight and weigh the net on a suspended spring-balance weighing scale. (Element 8.2.2)

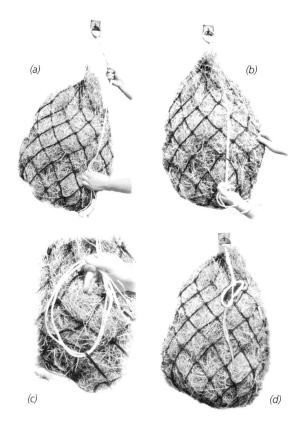

(a)

(b)

(c)

(d)

TYING UP A HAYNET.
(a) Pull the haynet tight up to the ring. (b) Pass the long string through the net as near to the bottom of the net as you can. Then (c)–(d) pull the string back up to keep the net high on the wall and secure with a slip knot.

- In tying up the net, pull the string right through the ring until the full net is tight up against the ring, then thread the extra string through the bottom of the haynet and pull the net up as high as you can again on the ring before securing the string. This ensures that even when the net is empty it does not hang low down the wall where the horse could get a foot caught in it and be injured. (Elements 8.2.3–8.2.4)

Horse Health

Know:

The signs of good health in horses and ponies. Recognise when they are off-colour and the importance of an immediate report.

ELEMENT

| S | **9.1.1** State what you must look for at morning inspections. |

| S | **9.1.2** State what you must look for at last thing at night inspections. |

| C | **9.2.1** Recognise signs of good health. |

| C | **9.2.2** Recognise signs of ill health. |

| C | **9.3.1** Give the reasons for reporting when a horse is unwell. |

What the examiner is looking for

- The ability to recognise good health in horse(s) is an essential and basic requirement for anyone involved in the care of and responsibility for horses. Your training should have covered the various points of good and ill health and you may have been involved in or seen senior yard staff taking horses' temperatures, pulse and respiration rates, as these can be clear guides to a horse's state of well being.

- If you are asked about early-morning inspections, the examiner would be looking for you to mention that the horse was demonstrating 'normal' behaviour. For example, you might report that the horse had eaten and drunk through the night; the stable looked 'normal', with droppings and bed disturbance no different to usual. The horse appeared at ease with himself, and greeted you over the door as you arrived, anxious for his breakfast. Everything in the stable, with the horse and in the vicinity of the yard, indicated that nothing untoward had happened during the night. (Element 9.1.1)

- Before leaving the yard at night (Element 9.1.2) last checks would include making sure that the horse(s) was comfortable with hay as required and a full water bucket. The horse(s) rugs might need to be adjusted or increased according to weather conditions. Final feeds may need to be given as necessary. If horses have worked then they must be left cooled off, brushed off and rugged up appropriately. All lights and electrical appliances must be turned off, the tack room securely locked and any security alarms etc. set. Before you leave, have a final glance to check round that everything is left safe and sound.

- You will be asked about signs of good health and ill health and these may relate to a horse in front of you. (Elements 9.2.1–9.2.2). On the whole, the signs of good health are the opposite of those showing illness:

  1. Bright eyes, no discharge from eyes, nose or mouth.

  2. Flexible, shiny coat.

  3. Horse at ease with himself (no uncomfortable stance or discomfort through limbs).

  4. No signs of gut pain (kicking stomach or pawing the ground).

  5. Eating and drinking normally.

  6. All body functions normal (clear urine, normal droppings). Temperature, pulse and respiration rates are all acceptable (respectively 100.5°F / 38°C, 36–44 beats per minute, 8–12 inhalations/exhalations per minute).

- Reporting any adverse signs as soon as possible would mean being able to deal with a developing problem at the earliest possible opportunity, thus limiting the chances of a serious complication arising. (Element 9.3.1)

Horse Behaviour

Show knowledge of:

The horse's natural lifestyle, instincts, actions and reactions.

| S | **10.1.1** Outline the horse's lifestyle in the wild. |

S **10.1.1** Outline the horse's lifestyle in the wild.

S **10.2.1** Describe the horse's basic instincts of survival.

C **10.3.1** Describe how to handle the horse in the stable.

C **10.3.2** Describe how to handle the horse in the field.

C **10.3.3** Describe how to handle the horse when ridden.

S **10.4.1** Describe signs of danger as shown in the horse's expression when in the field.

S **10.4.2** Describe signs of danger as shown in the horse's expression when in the stable.

S **10.4.3** Describe signs of danger as shown in the horse's expression when ridden.

What the examiner is looking for

- You should know that the horse is a herd animal, a herbivore (vegetarian/grass eating), and a gregarious creature who likes the company of other equines. His natural lifestyle would be to eat grass for most of the day, browsing and moving over the area available to him. (Element 10.1.1)

- His instinctive reactions are to run away from things that frighten him and not confront them. (Element 10.2.1) If something is restricting him and he cannot run, he may rear, or if something is disturbing his balance on his back, he may buck.

- Handling the horse requires ongoing awareness and understanding of how the horse is interacting with you. (Element 10.3.1) In the stable, always let the horse know where you are; never surprise him or touch him suddenly without him knowing you are there. Use your voice to warn him of your approach and then endeavour to pat him on his neck or shoulder before approaching to, for example, place a headcollar on him and tie him up. When handling the horse in the stable it is safer always to have him tied up, both for his safety and yours.

- When handling the horse in the field it is equally vital that he knows you are there or are approaching. If there are other horses loose in the field then be aware that they may all come towards you, out of interest. Be confident and firm as you approach the horse you need to catch/inspect/bring in etc. If you have visible food in a hand or pocket then the 'boss' of the field may chase the other horses away from you. To avoid such problems it may be wise to go with another person, especially if you are bringing in more than one horse/pony. Remember that putting a bridle on the horse would give more control than a headcollar.

- When riding the horse, again an awareness of its attitude and behaviour is essential. A nervous horse is tense, and may snort and refuse to go forward. He may gain confidence from having a braver, more confident horse take the lead. A positive, firm approach from you is essential to build the horse's confidence. If the horse is spooking at something, try to turn his head away from the object and ride him positively forward. If necessary, reduce the pace to improve your control, and use your voice to reassure him. (Element 10.3.3)

- Horses acting abnormally in a field will herd together. They may run around as a group (away from the perceived danger). (Element 10.4.1) Often, anxious horses have their heads high in the air; they look as if their eyes are 'out on stalks', their nostrils are flared and they may snort.

- Horses demonstrating signs of danger in the stable are unable to run away instinctively from the danger, so they sometimes 'hide' in the corner of the box. They tend to turn their backside towards the perceived danger, put their ears back flat on their necks and 'threaten' with their hind legs if you approach. (Element 10.4.2)

- Horses demonstrating signs of danger when ridden may rear if frightened in the mouth, may buck if fearful of the saddle or the rider in the saddle, and may spook and try to run away from things which frighten them. (Element 10.4.3)

Basic Grassland Care

Know:

What to look for in and around the field.

Daily inspections.

How to turn out a horse, how to catch him and bring him in from the field.

Recognise a horse-sick field.

ELEMENT

S **11.1.1** Describe a 'horse-sick' field.

S **11.1.2** Give ways a horse-sick field can be avoided/remedied.

C **11.2.1** Describe what to check each day in the field.

C **11.3.1** Describe acceptable, safe methods of turning a horse out into a field.

C **11.3.2** Describe acceptable, safe methods of bringing a horse in from the field.

What the examiner is looking for

- You must be able to discuss and describe a 'horse-sick' field. (Element 11.1.1) The examiner would expect you to know that the following would be indicative of 'horse-sick' pasture:

  1. Too many horses or ponies on a relatively small patch of land.

  2. Many piles of droppings scattered around the pasture.

Ragwort – this poisonous plant has yellow daisy-like, multi-headed flowers and serrated leaves.

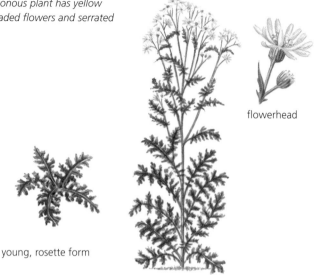

flowerhead

young, rosette form

3. Patches of smooth, well-grazed 'bowling green' areas of grass with few droppings interspersed by patches of lank, dark-green, long grass where the horses have fouled and will not eat the developing 'leggy' grass.

4. An abundance of nettles and docks and other hardy weeds (often ragwort) which deplete the grass and may be harmful to the horses.

5. Often 'horse-sick' pasture may also have neglected or unsuitable fencing around it.

- Horse-sick pasture can be avoided by good management. Rotation of paddocks gives the pasture a chance to rest and regrow and ensures that is not constantly overgrazed. Sensible stocking levels avoid putting too many horses on too small an area of grassland. Regular removal of droppings (preferably by picking them up by hand, removal with a vacuum-type machine or harrowing to spread them) alleviates the tendency for uneven and poor grazing patches to establish (some areas become overgrazed while others are covered in droppings and then a rank covering of untouched, tainted grass). Cross-grazing with other animals will also sweeten the pasture and reduce the risk of it becoming sick. (Element 11.1.2)

- Daily checks of pasture should include checking the fencing for safety and repair, noting the state of the grass, making sure that the gate is secure, and that shelter and water supply are in a good state. Keep a watchful eye for the appearance of any poisonous plants or dangerous objects which could harm the horses. (Element 11.2.1)

- When turning horses out, the safety of handler and horse is of paramount concern. Horses may be enthusiastic about returning to the field and therefore you must minimise the risk of being injured by their joy at returning to freedom. Always take enough people to manage the number of horses you are turning out, the number required depending on the horses' manner and behaviour. One person may easily turn out three or four quiet ponies, whereas it would be wise to have one person per horse with two or three fit, competition horses being turned out for some exercise. In general terms:

  1. Open the gate and make sure that all people and horses/ponies are in the field and the gate has been closed again.

  2. Make sure that the handlers are in their own space and that they have turned their horse(s) back to face the closed gate.

  3. Make sure that everyone releases their horse(s) at the same time, so that all the horses run off together – but first they have to make a turn. This avoids the tendency for them to kick up their heels (in your face) and run away violently.

  4. Make sure that the gate is securely closed as you leave. (Element 11.3.1)

- When bringing horses in from the field (Element 11.3.2), the same criteria would apply for numbers. The number of horses/ponies which can be safely managed depends extensively on the type and fitness of the animals and on the competence and experience of the handlers.

- An experienced person would be more able to manage several horses than an inexperienced, less-confident person.

- If taking food to entice the horse(s) be very careful that it does not incite a horse's natural instinctive reaction to display dominance or 'pecking order' traits.

- Food, if used, must be offered discreetly, as the horse is approached from the front but slightly towards the shoulder or neck. Introduce the rope of the headcollar around the horse's neck and then apply the headcollar, attaching the strap securely.

- Lead the horse(s) to the gate and bring them out, being careful to keep any remaining animals in the field and closing the gate securely. Bring horses in in an orderly way, not getting too close to each other and making sure that you have prepared somewhere for the horses to go when they come into the yard. (Element 11.3.2)

Watering and Feeding

General principles and the importance of cleanliness.

The various types of fodder in general use and recognise good and bad quality feed.

Suitable feeding of horses and ponies in light work.

(Definition of 'light work': daily walk, trot and canter where the horse is not stressed.)

ELEMENT

C	**12.1.1**	Name oats, barley, sugar-beet, bran, coarse mix, nuts/cubes, chaff.
S	**12.1.2**	Recognise good quality oats, barley, sugar-beet pulp/cubes, bran, coarse mix, nuts/cubes, chaff.
S	**12.1.3**	Recognise poor quality oats, barley, sugar-beet pulp/cubes, bran, coarse mix, nuts/cubes, chaff.
S	**12.2.1**	Recognise good quality hay.
S	**12.2.2**	Recognise bad quality hay.
S	**12.2.3**	Recognise acceptable quality hay.
S	**12.3.1**	Recognise good quality haylage.
S	**12.3.2**	Recognise bad quality haylage.
S	**12.4.1**	Discuss the dangers of feeding poor quality fodder.
C	**12.5.1**	Give the rules of good feeding.
C	**12.6.1**	Give the rules of watering.
S	**12.6.2**	Know the importance of cleanliness.

C **12.7.1** Discuss suitable feed for a grass-kept horse and/or pony in light work throughout the seasons.

S **12.7.2** Discuss suitable daily quantity of feed for a grass-kept horse and/or pony in light work throughout the seasons.

C **12.8.1** Discuss suitable feed for a stabled horse and/or pony in light work.

S **12.8.2** Discuss suitable daily quantity of feed for a stabled horse and/or pony in light work.

C **12.9.1** Discuss suitable methods of watering horses at grass.

S **12.9.2** Discuss suitable methods of feeding horses at grass.

What the examiner is looking for

- Try to make sure that you are familiar with recognising different types of feed in 'your' feed room, and in any other yard where you might have the chance to look at the feeds in use there.

- In the examination you may be handed feed samples in screw-top glass jars; some of these samples may have been there a long time, and if you do attempt to consider their smell and brightness, they may not live up to the quality you would hope for. Make sure you can identify a small sample of feed in a jam-jar, which may not look as clear as a large bin or sack full of the commodity.

- The feeds listed in Element 12.1.1 should be familiar to you.

- Quality of feed (Element 12.1.2) is identified by a pleasant smell, bright clear colour, no apparent dampness, mould or tainting with any foreign objects. The feed should look fresh, clean and palatable.

- Poor quality fodder (Element 12.1.3) would be the opposite of the above: unpleasant smell, mouldy or musty, poor colour, and overall appearance would be unacceptable and unpalatable.

- Recognising good and poor quality hay (Elements 12.2.1–12.2.3) is important. It involves the sweetness of the smell of the hay, bright colour, clean flexible stalks with well-defined leaves and some flower or seed heads. Dust and mould in the hay is unacceptable as it may cause digestive problems due to the toxins present in mould. Hay which smells musty would probably be rejected by the horse. Acceptable hay may not have the sweetness and brightness of good hay but would still be dust- and mould-free and as such should not disadvantage the horse if eaten.

- Recognition of the quality of haylage (Elements 12.3.1–12.3.2) is similar to that of hay. Haylage is cut from a younger crop of grass and is preserved with a higher moisture content than hay. Good-quality haylage will smell more pungent than hay, and will also be much 'damper' in its texture. Nevertheless it should not have any mould or unpleasant smell. Haylage needs to be used fairly swiftly (within three to five days, depending on the weather) after opening its vacuum-sealed bag, or it will begin to decompose and may then be unsuitable to feed.

- Feeding poor-quality fodder of any kind may lead to illness, particularly digestive problems. The horse may be put off his food if the quality is poor and then he may become a picky feeder which, again, can cause digestive problems. Feeding poor-quality fodder is a false economy because the horse may be ill, off work and require veterinary attention. (Element 12.4.1)

- Learn the rules for feeding so that you know them off by heart. (Element 12.5.1) They are the foundation from which you will feed horses of all types throughout your time of working with and caring for equines. Rules for feeding should include:

  1. Feed little and often. The horse has a small stomach and feeding little and often mimics his natural grazing pattern as much as possible.

  2. Feed according to size, age, body weight, type, temperament, type of work to be expected of the horse and the level of rider who will be riding him.

  3. Always feed good quality fodder (as explained above).

  4. Feed plenty of bulk – this, again, keeps him as close to his natural lifestyle as possible.

  5. Always feed from clean utensils or bowls.

  6. Make sure the horse has a constant access to a clean supply of fresh water. He

should then not choose to gulp down large quantities of water immediately after a feed.

7. Feed at least an hour before exercise, and longer before demanding work. After a feed the stomach is full and may restrict lung expansion when the horse exerts himself in work. Also there is not a conflict within the horse's system trying both to digest food and produce energy for muscular action.

8. Feed at regular times daily – horses are creatures of habit and thrive on routine.

9. Feed something succulent every day – this helps keep the stabled horse happy and healthy.

- Rules for watering. (Element 12.6.1) The horse should have constant access to a clean supply of fresh water at all times, whether stabled or at grass. Be familiar with the methods of how this might be provided (e.g. water buckets, self-filling bowls, water troughs, etc.) and the pros and cons of some of these. Make sure that you refer to regular cleaning of water carriers and learn to be aware of knowing how much horses in your care drink, on average, on a daily basis.

- The importance of cleanliness (Element 12.6.2) follows on from the provision of fresh water in clean utensils. Cleanliness refers not only to watering but to feeding as well. Cleanliness is of the utmost importance in any well-run riding establishment. Maintaining cleanliness is in the interests of all the horse's health and well-being and is likely to inhibit the proliferation of vermin.

- Assessing how much feed to give a horse comes with practice, but first you need to understand the basic concept that the horse, when left to his own devices in the field and not asked to work, will eat 100% bulk (grass or hay). When we start to work him, the horse needs extra nutrients in his feed to give him the energy to sustain the work. If he is in light work only, i.e. he is not being put under stress to work hard, he will need only a small percentage of concentrate food, perhaps 90–80% bulk to 10–20% concentrate. As an example, let's consider a horse of about 16hh, weighing about 450kg/1000lb and in light/medium work (Element 12.8.2). This horse would be capable of eating between 11.25kg and 13.5kg (25lb and 30lb) of food per day (based on a requirement of 2.5–3% of his bodyweight in food daily). Assuming he needs about 80% bulk, then we are looking at about 10kg (22lb) of bulk per day and about 2.75–3.5kg (6–8lb) concentrate (say, 3.25kg/7lb). Since the horse is in light/medium work, it is probably easiest to feed him twice a day. In the morning he could have 1.5kg (3lb) concentrate with 2.25kg (5lb) hay; at lunch time he could have 2.25kg (5lb) hay and no concentrate; at night he could have a 1.75kg (4lb) feed with about 5.5kg (12lb) hay to last overnight.

■ You might choose to feed the horse either cubes or a coarse mix. Being 'complete' feeds this would ensure that all the right nutrients were present. (Element 12.8.1) This can make feeding much less complicated. You might also choose to add a little sugar-beet as a succulent, and some alfalfa chaff to slow down the horse's rate of eating and improve his chewing.

■ If the horse/pony is living at grass (Elements 12.7.1–12.7.2) then his requirements will be greater in the winter when there is little or no nutritive value in the grass. The winter grass still provides him with a fibrous mass to chew, but this would need to be supplemented by hay. If there is frost or snow on the ground then more hay would be fed, cutting down as the weather improved. As the grass starts to grow again the horse/pony (even in light work) may need little or no supplementary feeding. Suitable concentrate feeds for horses/ponies at grass are cubes or coarse mix. If ponies are inclined to lose weight in winter then barley may help to maintain their condition.

■ While the horse/pony at grass derives much water content from the grass he eats, nevertheless constant access to a source of fresh, clean water is essential. Knowledge of different methods of watering would be expected (Element 12.9.1). These might include a self-filling water trough, fresh running stream, or a refillable plastic tub. Some knowledge of the advantages and disadvantages of these and any other methods would be appropriate.

■ Knowledge of suitable methods of feeding horses and ponies at grass (Element 12.9.2) is expected. Discuss how 'pecking order' affects group feeding, creating a need for horses to be fed with the food source well spread out to prevent one horse bullying others. Consider the merits or otherwise of piles of hay on the floor, haynets tied to the fence, and individual bowls/buckets for each animal.

General Knowledge

Know:

The risks and responsibilities involved when riding or leading on the public highway.

The correct procedures in the event of an accident. Safety rules and fire precautions.

The British Horse Society's aims.

ELEMENT

C	**13.1.1**	Describe suitable clothes to wear when working with horses.
C	**13.2.1**	Describe fire precautions in the work place.
C	**13.3.1**	Give the correct procedure in the event of an accident to a person.
S	**13.4.1**	Give the safety rules for riding in a class.
C	**13.4.2**	Give the rules and good manners involved when taking horses on the public highway.
S	**13.5.1**	Give the aims of The British Horse Society.

What the examiner is looking for

- You should know that safe footwear is of paramount importance when working around horses. Sturdy shoes or boots (never soft shoes or trainers) are what is needed. Flapping or loose fashion clothing is unsuitable. Gloves and riding hats are an added precaution when handling young or unruly horses. Jewellery should be minimal (a watch and wedding ring) or preferably not worn at all. Avoid strong perfume, which can excite horses. You should be warm, dry and able to move easily in whatever you wear. In the working environment you should look neat, tidy and professional. (Element 13.1.1)

- Everyone working in the establishment should be briefed in fire precautions and fire drill for the centre. These should include a strict 'no smoking' policy anywhere in the yard. There should be fire extinguishers in small areas, such as the tack room and office, and fire-fighting equipment, such as hoses permanently attached to a water supply, for large areas of the yard. There should be an alarm, to which everyone reacts, and a system for quickly turning horses out into nearby paddocks in the event of a fire. Everyone should have a clear understanding of how to call the fire brigade. (Element 13.2.1)

- Feel very sure that you could carry out an acceptable procedure in the event of someone in your yard suffering an accident:

  1. Remain calm.

  2. Assess the situation and go first to the injured person (call for assistance if you think you may need it – but you should not be in sole charge at this level).

  3. Encourage the casualty to stay still and not hurry to get up (he or she may be winded, shocked or even have broken a limb).

  4. Reassure the person; if necessary, keep them warm with a coat or blanket and encourage them to breathe deeply and stay still.

  5. Follow the instructions of the person in charge.

  6. Know how to call an ambulance if one is necessary. In the UK that means dialling 999. Give the location as clearly as you can and a brief explanation of the accident and casualty.

  7. After the incident has been dealt with, make sure that when the accident book is completed, you sign the record as being a witness to the incident, checking that everything is clearly and correctly recorded. This should be done as soon after the accident as possible.

- When riding in a class lesson you should always mount safely, preferably with everyone in an orderly line so that the horses are well spaced and no horse can interfere with another. Whether riding in closed or open order, make sure that you never get too close to another horse. If you have to pass another horse from any direction, always allow enough space and try not to take another horse and rider by surprise. If in doubt, let them know you are close. Always pass other riders left hand to left hand, and give way to a faster pace, i.e. if you are in walk then give way to a rider coming behind you in trot. If one rider is having trouble with his horse, give him extra space until he has regained his control and calmness. If there is an incident where a rider falls off, the whole ride should halt until the problem is resolved. (Element 13.4.1)

- Rules and good manners involved with taking horses on the public highway (Element 13.4.2) would include:

1. Always be aware of and courteous to other road users.

2. Thank anyone who slows down for you. Acknowledge with a smile or nod, even if you cannot take your hand off the reins.

3. Be aware of what is going on around you. Make clear signals to others as to your intentions.

4. Wear fluorescent clothing and equipment on yourself and your horse so that you are easily visible to other road users.

HAND SIGNALS

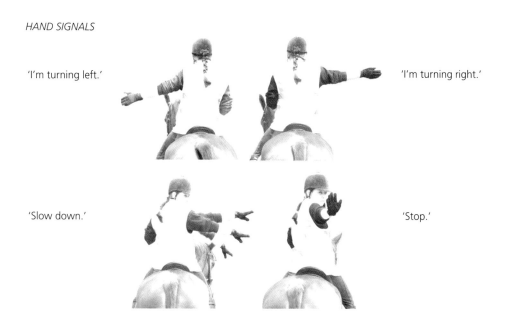

'I'm turning left.'

'I'm turning right.'

'Slow down.'

'Stop.'

Check behind for traffic before moving out to pass a parked car.

If leading on the road, the horse must wear a bridle. Place yourself between the horse and the traffic, and lead in the same direction as the traffic. Always wear high-visibility gear.

5. Ride carefully, in single file, unless the road is wide enough and the visibility is good enough for it to be safe to use double file.

6. Never ride on a pavement or footpath (it is illegal to do so in the UK). If there are pedestrians nearby, they may be frightened by the size of the horse.

7. Never ride on ornamental grass verges or on any areas where someone has obviously taken trouble to maintain the grass in lawn condition.

8. If leading a horse on the highway, it must wear a bridle. You should place yourself between the horse and the traffic, leading it in the same direction as the traffic is travelling (i.e. in the UK that would mean leading on the left-hand side of the road with you on the right-hand side of the horse).

- You should know that The British Horse Society is the biggest charity membership organisation whose aims are the interests and welfare of the horse. (Element 13.5.1) The Society works hard in the following areas:

1. Welfare.

2. Education and training, including administering the examination system which regulates instructor qualifications.

3. Safety.

4. Rights of way and access.

5. The BHS approves riding schools and livery yards across the UK and abroad.

6. The BHS has a nationwide system of British Riding Clubs which are affiliated to the Society.

Stage 1
Riding

Syllabus

Candidates are required to demonstrate their ability to ride a quiet, experienced horse or pony in an enclosed space without assistance. their balance and security should indicate the correct foundation for future progress.

Candidates who are considered to be well below the standard may be asked to retire.

IMPORTANT: Candidates are advised to check that they are working from the latest examination syllabus, as examination content and procedure are liable to alteration. Contact the BHS Examinations Office for up-to-date information regarding the syllabus.

British Horse Society – Stage 1 Syllabus

Stage 1- Riding

Candidates must be physically fit in order to carry out the selected tasks and topics efficiently without undue stress and strain and they will be expected to demonstrate competent use of time.

Candidates are required to demonstrate their ability to ride a quiet, experienced horse or pony in an enclosed space without assistance. Their balance and security should indicate the correct foundation for future progress. *Candidates who are considered to be well below the standard may be asked to retire.*

Unit code number S1RIDI

Learning Outcomes	Element	Assessment criteria	
RIDING The candidate should be able to;		The candidate has achieved this outcome because s/he can:	**Influence**
	1.1.1	Demonstrate safe, effective leading in hand at walk	Compulsory
Demonstrate; Leading a saddled	1.2.1	Demonstrate safe, effective leading in hand at trot	Supporting
and bridled horse in hand, from either side.	1.3.1	Demonstrate safe, correct turning of the horse when leading in hand	Compulsory
Checking saddlery for its fitting and soundness.	1.4.1	Carryout appropriate tack checking procedures prior to mounting	Supporting
Demonstrate; Mounting and	2.1.1	Demonstrate correct mounting from a mounting block	Compulsory
dismounting from the ground, and from a mounting block.	2.2.1	Demonstrate correct mounting from the ground	Supporting
	2.3.1	Demonstrate correct dismounting	Compulsory
Demonstrate; Taking up and adjusting stirrups and reins.	3.1.1	Carry out correct girth adjusting procedures prior to riding away	Compulsory
Checking and tightening girths.	3.2.1	Carry out correct stirrup adjusting procedures prior to riding away	Compulsory
	3.3.1	Demonstrate correct placement of stirrup leathers	Supporting
	3.4.1	Demonstrate correct method of holding the rein	Supporting
Show, the correct basics in the ability to maintain a correct,	4.1.1	Show a correct, secure and balanced position at walk with stirrups at a suitable length for riding on the flat	Compulsory
balanced position when riding with stirrups	4.2.1	Show a correct, secure and balanced position at trot with stirrups at a suitable length for riding on the flat	Compulsory
	4.3.1	Show a correct, secure and balanced position at canter with stirrups at a suitable length for riding on the flat	Supporting
Show, the correct basics in the ability to maintain a correct,	5.1.1	Show a correct, secure and balanced position at walk without stirrups	Compulsory
balanced position when riding without stirrups	5.2.1	Show a correct, secure and balanced position at trot without stirrups	Compulsory
Show, the correct basics in the ability to maintain a correct, balanced position in preparation	6.1.1	Maintain a correct, secure and balanced position at the rising trot and in the jumping seat with stirrups at a suitable length	Compulsory
for jumping	6.2.1	Maintain a correct, secure and balanced position at the canter in the jumping seat with stirrups at a suitable length	Supporting
Show, the correct basics in the ability to maintain a correct, balanced position when working over poles.	7.1.1	Demonstrate a correct, secure and balanced position at the trot in the light balanced jumping seat with stirrups at a suitable length over ground poles	Compulsory
Show, a basic understanding of the natural aids.	8.1.1	Demonstrate the natural aids for riding the horse forward correctly	Compulsory
	8.2.1	Demonstrate the natural aids for riding correct circles	Supporting
	8.3.1	Demonstrate the natural aids for riding correct turns	Supporting
	8.4.1	Demonstrate the natural aids for riding correct straight lines	Supporting
Know, the reasons for trotting on named diagonals.	9.1.1	Demonstrate an ability to rise with correct diagonals	Supporting
Know an incorrect leading leg in canter and trot to enable a correct	10.1.1	Demonstrate an ability to recognise cantering with the correct leading leg	Compulsory
lead to be established.	10.1.2	Uses corners/ half circles to help ensure correct strike-offs into canter	Compulsory
Know how to handle the reins	11.1.1	Show a correctly maintained rein contact throughout	Supporting
Know how to handle a whip	12.1.1	Demonstrate correct use of a whip which does not exceed 75 centimetres (30 inches)	Supporting

Riding

Leading a saddled and bridled horse in hand, from either side.

Checking saddlery for its fitting and soundness.

ELEMENT

C	**1.1.1**	Demonstrate safe, effective leading in hand at walk.
S	**1.2.1**	Demonstrate safe, effective leading in hand at trot.
C	**1.3.1**	Demonstrate safe, correct turning of the horse when leading in hand.
S	**1.4.1**	Carry out appropriate tack-checking procedures prior to mounting.

What the examiner is looking for

- We have discussed leading the horse in hand in the care section (pages 43-45) and all the same principles apply here. (Elements 1.1.1, 1.2.1 and 1.3.1)

- It is necessary that you are competent in leading the horse from both sides as there may be a requirement for you to lead the horse on a public highway at

Leading the horse in hand. The stirrups are run up and the reins taken over the horse's head.

Leading in hand. This horse is wearing a running martingale so the leader leaves the reins over the neck and leads as shown.

some time. In this latter case you would lead the horse on the nearside of the road, placing yourself between the traffic and the horse (i.e. leading the horse on the offside) (see page 66). When you are leading a horse in a bridle, take the reins over the head (unless the horse is wearing a martingale, in which case you would lead with the reins in place around the horse's neck). If leading for some distance make sure that the girth is firm and the stirrups are run up and cannot slip down.

■ Before mounting, check the girth and tighten it a little, if necessary. Make sure that the reins are over the horse's head ready to mount, and at that point just check that the bridle looks comfortable and the horse is at ease. Pull down the

Incorrectly fitted bridle – bit too low, browband pinching the base of the ears, and noseband too high and pressing against the cheekbone.

Incorrectly fitted bridle – bit too high, browband pinching the base of the ears, and noseband too high and pressing against the cheekbone.

The bridle looks comfortable for the horse: the bit just wrinkles the corner of the mouth, the noseband is about two fingers' width below the cheekbone, and the browband allows room around the base of the ears.

stirrups so that they are ready for use when mounting – you can roughly estimate your stirrup length by putting the iron up under your armpit. Check the stirrups from in front of the horse to see that they are hanging level.

Estimating stirrup length. Keep a loose hold on the reins or put your arm through them while carrying out this procedure, unless the horse is tied up or being held by someone else.

Demonstrate:

Mounting and dismounting from the ground and from a mounting block.

ELEMENT

C   **2.1.1** Demonstrate correct mounting from a mounting block.

S   **2.2.1** Demonstrate correct mounting from the ground.

What the examiner is looking for

- Mounting correctly and well is in the interests of the horse's welfare as well as your own. It is a very important part of developing skill as a rider. You should have been taught to mount well and correctly at the outset of your riding experience, and this skill should stay with you throughout your riding life. There will be many occasions (particularly for older riders) when it is appropriate to mount using a mounting block, but nevertheless the ability to mount in an agile way, not inconveniencing the horse, should be of paramount importance. If we discuss some of the reasons why mounting is so important, this will give you a clear idea of why examiners consider competence in this (perhaps small) part of the Stage 1 exam to be of high value. (Elements 2.1.1 and 2.2.1)

If you learn to mount athletically and well, the horse will benefit in the following ways:

- You will unbalance him less because you are agile and in control of your body weight.

- You will spring up from the ground and lower your weight gently into the saddle.

- You will avoid ever touching him with your right leg as it passes over his rump.

- By springing up and putting your hand well onto the offside of the saddle, you will avoid pulling the saddle towards you and risking the saddle slipping or the

Mounting from the ground.

reins short enough to control
horse and prevent him moving off;
right hand holds the stirrup

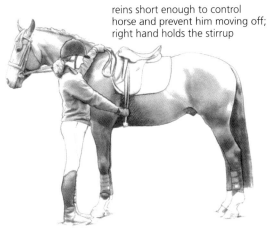

right hand must go well over
to the offside of the saddle

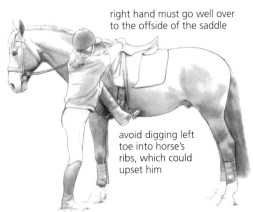

avoid digging left
toe into horse's
ribs, which could
upset him

right leg must clear the
horse's quarters athletically;
weight must be lowered, with
control, lightly into the saddle

tree being twisted by the strain put onto it.

- You are less likely to cause the horse to tense and dip away from your weight, or, worse still, to tighten his back and try to run away or buck as you sit down on him.

Poor mounting technique can ultimately injure the horse's back, damage the saddle, damage the rider's back, and create tension and an unsettled reaction in the horse, which could cause an accident.

- Whether mounting from the ground or from a mounting block the same principles apply. From a mounting block there is obviously less need to spring. The horse should stand still while you mount (if necessary, the horse should be held by the mounting block); otherwise you must keep the reins short enough in your left rein to control the horse and keep him still.

Demonstrate:

Taking up and adjusting stirrups and reins.

Checking and tightening girths.

ELEMENT

C	**3.1.1**	Carry out correct girth adjusting procedures prior to riding away.
S	**3.2.1**	Carry out correct stirrup adjusting procedures prior to riding away.
S	**3.3.1**	Demonstrate correct placement of stirrup leathers.
S	**3.4.1**	Demonstrate correct method of holding the rein.

What the examiner is looking for

- Once mounted, you should be proficient in checking your girth from the saddle and able to ease the girth to tighten it. Slide your leg well forward and keep your reins short so that you can control the horse; stay relaxed and balanced as you pull up the saddle flap to expose the girth straps. If there is a buckle guard, make sure it is pulled down smoothly over the buckles once you have tightened the girth. (Element 3.1.1) If, after riding around for a few minutes, you feel the girth needs a final check and adjustment, then ask to turn in and recheck it.

Tightening the girth whilst in the saddle.

Adjusting the stirrup length whilst in the saddle. Throughout the rider keeps his/her feet in the irons for security.

- Your stirrups should be level. Hang your leg alongside the stirrup and the base of the stirrup iron should be in the vicinity of your ankle bone. If your stirrups need adjusting then do this with your foot loosely in the iron, pull the leather up and then use the pressure of your foot on the iron to slide the leather back into place. (Element 3.2.1) If, after riding for a few minutes, your stirrups feel unlevel or too short/long then ask if you may turn in and change them You must feel comfortable. Learning to ride with a stirrup that feels 'right' for you takes time and 'feel'. If you are nervous or tense then you are less likely to 'let down' into your stirrups as well as on a day when you feel confident and relaxed. Whenever you are anxious (e.g. on the first horse in your exam) it may be wise to have your stirrups one hole shorter than 'normal'. It is easy to let the stirrups down as you relax. If you start with them over-long you may look loose and insecure in your riding.

- The stirrup leathers should lie flat along your leg. (Element 3.3.1) If you inadvertently have a turn in the leather, then the edge of the stirrup leather will lie against your leg, and usually feels uncomfortable.

Correct holding of the reins. Hands level, and thumbs uppermost with wrists relaxed.

- Pick up the reins smoothly and with feel. The reins should be held one in each hand, with the hands level; the thumbs should be on the top of the rein with the fingers closed around the rein; the wrists and elbows should be relaxed, and there should be an imaginary line from the elbow, through the forearm, through the rein to the horse's mouth, so that an even contact is sustained on the reins. (Element 3.4.1)

Show:

The correct basics in the ability to maintain a correct, balanced position when riding with stirrups.

ELEMENT

C **4.1.1** Show a correct, secure and balanced position at walk with stirrups at a suitable length for riding on the flat.

C **4.2.1** Show a correct, secure and balanced position at trot with stirrups at a suitable length for riding on the flat.

S **4.3.1** Show a correct, secure and balanced position at canter with stirrups at a suitable length for riding on the flat.

What the examiner is looking for

- The correct basics **MUST** be seen. (Elements 4.1.1, 4.2.1 and 4.3.1.) The basic balanced position – the rider sitting centrally in the saddle, the weight evenly on

The correct position for the rider, as seen from the side. Notice the shoulder–hip–heel alignment.

both seat bones, an imaginary straight line running ear–shoulder–hip–heel, the rider demonstrating balance over the lower leg from a secure seat – is essential. The hand position already described adds a dimension of balance and harmony in that the rider is 'with' the horse and able to follow the basic movements and influence the horse's pace and direction.

- Work to develop the basic riding position on the flat: it is the foundation of your riding future. The more smoothly you can move from one pace to another whilst sustaining balance and position, the better.

Show:

The correct basics in the ability to maintain a correct, balanced position when riding without stirrups.

ELEMENT

C	**5.1.1** Show a correct, secure and balanced position at walk without stirrups.
C	**5.2.1** Show a correct, secure and balanced position at trot without stirrups.

What the examiner is looking for

- The whole development of your riding is based on your basic position and balance. This enables you to control and influence your horse safely and effectively.

- Moving from one pace to another will constantly demonstrate your balance and co-ordination, which must be secure and harmonious.

- There is a need for you to look in harmony with the horse, and your ability to 'feel' how the horse is reacting to you must become an intrinsic part of your riding.

- Gripping up with the lower leg without stirrups, particularly in trot, is a common indicator that your balance is not well established and that you then rely on tightening the lower leg to stay on the horse. Aim to develop your suppleness and relaxation so that you can continually let your legs relax and lengthen around the horse.

- Maintain a straight position in the saddle, be careful not to tip inwards or allow your seat to slip to one side of the saddle. Your regular teacher should work with you to ensure that you are consistently sitting straight in the saddle. Crookedness will eventually have an adverse effect on the horse and will inhibit your ability to develop your riding with level influence.

- Make sure that you feel very confident about working without stirrups in walk and trot. Although you will not be asked to canter without stirrups in your exam, it is well worth your while being able to do so. Then when you are required to demonstrate only walk and trot, you will be working well within your level of competence.

Show:

The correct basics in the ability to maintain a correct, balanced position in preparation for jumping.

ELEMENT

| C | **6.1.1** Maintain a correct, secure and balanced position at the trot in the light, balanced jumping seat with stirrups at a suitable length. |

| S | **6.2.1** Maintain a correct, secure and balanced position at the canter in the jumping seat with stirrups at a suitable length. |

What the examiner is looking for

- You need to feel equally confident about riding at your 'normal flat length' and at 'jumping position length'. You must develop the ability to move from jumping position to upright position and back again, with no loss of balance to yourself and no loss of harmony or rhythm in the horse.

- Adopt a stirrup length one or two holes shorter than your 'flat' length, and from this be able to demonstrate a balance of your body weight distributed between the lower leg and the lighter seat. The angles between the lower leg and knee, and the thigh and upper body, are more closed as the rider takes the upper body a little forward, while still securely supported over the lower leg. The seat moves a little back in the saddle and the rider adopts a shorter rein length with the reins either side of the horse's neck. The rider looks up and the back is flat with the shoulders back. The seat is neither raised out of the saddle nor sitting down, as in the dressage seat position.

Jumping position. You must ride in balance. At faster paces, e.g. galloping across country, the upper body may be more forward than in a basic jumping position.

- You must feel confident to adopt the jumping position in walk, trot and canter around the school, either as an individual exercise or in open order. (Elements 6.1.1 and 6.2.1)

*Jumping position, with the rider's weight
absorbed through the lower leg, and the seat
just 'breathing' on the saddle.*

*Standing up in the stirrups – an exercise to help
riders find balance over their lower leg security.*

- Learn to 'stand up in your stirrups' as this is an exercise which helps you develop balance and security in the jumping position.

Show:

The correct basics in the ability to maintain a correct, balanced position when working over poles.

ELEMENT

 7.1.1 Demonstrate a correct, secure, and balanced position at the trot in the light, balanced jumping seat with stirrups at a suitable length over ground poles.

What the examiner is looking for

- You will be required to trot over trotting poles, either on the long side of the arena or on one or both diagonal lines of the school. You must be able to:

  1. Ride a good corner and maintain a good line of approach to the poles.

  2. Adopt a good, balanced jumping position just before the poles and maintain it through the poles and for a stride or two away.

Trotting over poles – the rider showing a balanced jumping position and a straight line through the poles.

3. Ride a good, straight line of departure away from the poles to a well-ridden corner and back onto the outside track.

4. Control the speed and activity of the horse so that he can maintain a clear rhythm through the poles.

5. Demonstrate an independent position that is never reliant on the reins for balance.

6. Demonstrate suppleness and good balance in harmony with the horse.

7. Maintain distances or ride independently to the poles as required.

Show:

A basic understanding of the natural aids.

ELEMENT

C	**8.1.1**	Demonstrate the natural aids for riding the horse forward correctly.
S	**8.2.1**	Demonstrate the natural aids for riding correct circles.
S	**8.3.1**	Demonstrate the natural aids for riding correct turns.
S	**8.4.1**	Demonstrate the natural aids for riding correct straight lines.

What the examiner is looking for

- Be very clear in your own mind about the basic aids for control. Very simply:

  - The rider's inside leg sends the horse forward and creates impulsion; it motivates the horse's inside hind leg and assists in helping the horse to be flexible on turns, circles and any line which is not straight.

- The rider's outside leg, usually slightly further back than the 'on the girth' position of the inside leg, also assists in forward movement, but specifically controls the hindquarters and prevents them from swinging out, encouraging them to 'follow' the front legs on turns and circles.

  - The rider's inside hand creates a slight flexion in the horse's head and neck (gullet) but never greater than the bend through the rest of the body.

  - The rider's outside hand controls the speed of the pace and also regulates the bend created by the inside rein.

- You must clearly demonstrate an ability to use these basic aids to produce independent forward movement (not just following another horse) on straight lines, turns and circles. (Elements 8.1.1, 8.2.1, 8.3.1 and 8.4.1)

- You must be able to ride accurate and active turns and circles (20m).

- You must be able to ride forward to halt and maintain immobility in halt.

- All this work must show not only that you have the ability to influence the horse

SCHOOL FIGURES

| *Change of rein down the centre line or across the school (B–E).* | *Change of rein across the diagonal.* | *Change of rein through half 10m circles and back to the track.* |

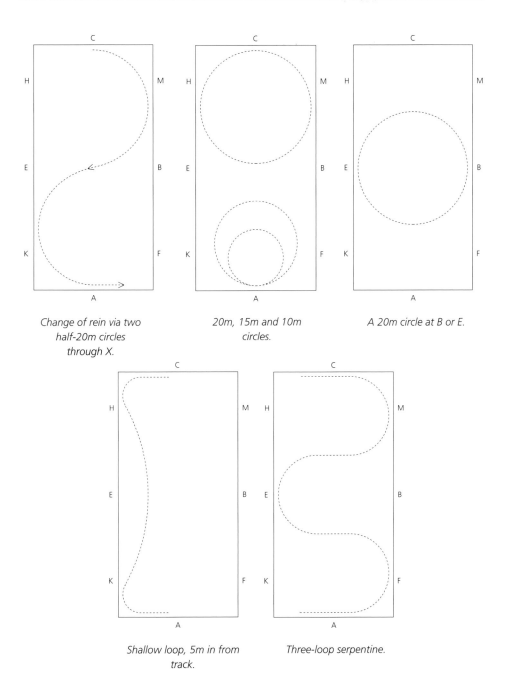

Change of rein via two half-20m circles through X.

20m, 15m and 10m circles.

A 20m circle at B or E.

Shallow loop, 5m in from track.

Three-loop serpentine.

effectively through basic figures, but also that your position is sufficiently secure and established to be able to ride the horse and movements without any dependence on the reins to maintain your balance. (Elements 4 and 5)

Practise riding turns and circles in many different situations in the school. Think of how many different places you can ride a 20m circle and practise it in walk, trot and canter, with and without your stirrups and in rising and sitting trot. Practise riding turns and inclines across the school, sometimes changing the rein through a turn and sometimes staying on the same rein. Practise all this work in closed order in a ride and also in open order.

Know:

The reasons for trotting on named diagonals.

ELEMENT

 9.1.1 Demonstrate an ability to rise with correct diagonals.

What the examiner is looking for

- You must be entirely familiar with the concept of diagonals in trot, their use and their value to you and the horse.

- Diagonals exist in trot because the trot pace is two-time and the legs move in diagonal pairs.

- The diagonals are named from the front legs (left diagonal is the left foreleg with the right hind leg; the right diagonal is the right foreleg with the left hind leg.)

- It is in the interests of the balance and suppleness of both horse and rider to ride on both diagonals in rising trot, so that the work is even on both reins.

- It is usual to ride on the outside diagonal, i.e. to sit in the saddle as the outside diagonal is on the ground. (On the left rein this means you ride on the right diagonal, and on the right rein you ride on the left diagonal.)

- For simplicity it is easier to refer to the 'inside' and 'outside' diagonal rather than

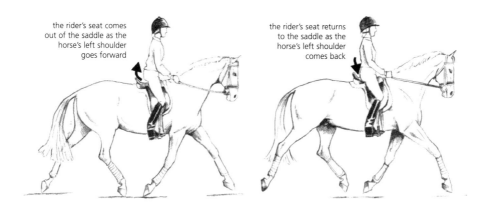

the rider's seat comes out of the saddle as the horse's left shoulder goes forward

the rider's seat returns to the saddle as the horse's left shoulder comes back

Riding on a specific diagonal in trot. Here the rider is on the left diagonal.

the left and right diagonal. Confusion can arise if you are on the right rein and an instructor tells you that you are on the 'right' diagonal (meaning the correct or outside diagonal) when you think you are on the left diagonal (which is in fact the one you are on!).

- Become familiar with changing the diagonal by sitting for one extra beat (step).

- Become familiar with knowing which diagonal you are on. First, glance at the horse's shoulders and decide which shoulder is coming back as you are sitting in the saddle. When the shoulder comes back, the same foot is on the floor; when the shoulder moves forward, the foot is in the air.

- Eventually you will develop feel for which diagonal you are on, but this takes time and practice. Some horses give you a clearer 'feel' than others. If in doubt, check by glancing down – do this with your eyes only. Do not allow your whole upper body to be affected by leaning forward.

- If you are in rising trot remember to change diagonal every time you change the direction, e.g. in changes of rein, in serpentine loops and on any occasion when there is a sustained change of the horse's bend.

- The occasional incorrect diagonal during your exam will not cause you to 'fail'. Only if you show a total lack of awareness or understanding of the use of diagonals on both the horses that you ride, is this likely to be considered an area which is not up to the standard required by a Stage 1 rider.

Know:

An incorrect leading leg in canter and trot to enable a correct lead to be established.

ELEMENT

C **10.1.1** Demonstrate an ability to recognise cantering with the correct leading leg.

C **10.1.2** Use corners/half circles to help ensure correct strike-offs into canter.

What the examiner is looking for

- Understanding the reason why horses canter on a 'leading leg' is essential at this level. You must feel very familiar with the fact that:

  - In canter the horse's legs move in three-time.

  - The sequence of horse's legs in canter is:

    outside hind leg forms the first beat,

    outside foreleg with the inside hind leg forms the second beat,

    inside foreleg forms the third beat,

    and then there is a moment of suspension when all four legs are off the ground at the same time.

- Naturally the horse is likely to give this sequence of legs whenever he canters unhindered and in balance, particularly on a curved line.

- We call the third beat of the canter the 'leading leg' because it appears to strike out in advance of the outside foreleg and 'lead' the canter.

- Remember, the way you apply the aids for a canter transition will help the horse to strike off on the correct leading leg.

- Ensure that the horse is in a balanced active trot before asking for canter.

- Ask for canter in a corner or on a half circle as this will encourage the horse to offer the correct lead.

- Apply your inside leg on the girth, your outside leg behind the girth, while maintaining the bend with the inside rein and controlling the pace with the outside rein.

- Try to develop 'feel' for the horse giving you the correct lead in canter. If he strikes off on the 'wrong' leg, try to feel the discomfort to you as the rider and the lack of balance that the horse is demonstrating.

- If you 'look' for the leading leg, make quite sure that you only use your eyes – taking the body forward to look, often unbalances the horse further and may actually encourage him to strike off on the wrong leg. (Elements 10.1.1 and 10.1.2)

An incorrect canter lead will not cause you to 'fail' your Stage 1 exam. Several incorrect leads, of which you appear to have no awareness, coupled with poor preparation for canter transitions and no correction of the fault when it occurs, are more likely to contribute to the examiner deciding that your competence is not yet sufficient for Stage 1.

Know:

How to handle the reins.

ELEMENT

S **11.1.1** Show a correctly maintained rein contact throughout.

What the examiner is looking for

- This element covers an overall observation of you as a rider. You should aim to maintain a consistent and 'feeling' contact with the horse through the rein in all your work. At no time should the rein be in loops (unless you are walking on a loose rein!) with no connection to the horse's mouth; conversely the rein should not be over-short and demonstrate tension and restriction, to which the horse is likely to show resistance.

- Your aim is to become a feeling rider with security in your position so that your balance is independent of the reins at all times. You can then work to develop a fluent, communicative, active rein contact throughout all your work.

- Work on your basic position. It is from a depth of seat and independence that a consistent rein contact is established.

Know:

How to handle a whip.

ELEMENT

 12.1.1 Demonstrate correct use of a whip which does not exceed 75cms (30ins).

What the examiner is looking for

- In holding and using a whip you must always show co-ordination and judgement.

- Handling of the whip while mounting, and in your basic riding, will be observed. At no time should the whip inconvenience you or the horse. You must learn to handle it carefully and efficiently when mounting and dismounting (whip in left hand), and learn to change it over smoothly by taking the reins into one hand when you change the direction. The whip should usually be carried in your inside hand where it supports the inside leg.

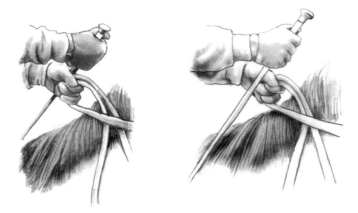

Changing the whip. Take the reins into one hand (the hand holding the whip), use the free hand to take the whip smoothly over the wither (as shown), then re-take both reins.

- If the horse is lazy to your leg or ignores your leg, the reins should be taken in one hand and the whip used smartly behind your inside leg on the horse's flank. There should be a reaction; the whip should not be used repeatedly in an aimless way because your leg does not have sufficient effect.

Questions and Answers

The following are a sample of the questions, along with suggested answers, which are regularly used in BHS exams by examiners. They are taken from *The British Horse Society's Examinations Handbook*.

Horse Behaviour

Q. What is the horse's natural lifestyle?
A. Herd animal. Constantly browsing and grazing. Living in a group of other horses, where a 'pecking order' is likely to develop.

Q. Name some instincts of the horse.
A. Flight (runs away from something fearful). Feeding. Breeding. Sixth sense, which creates a reaction for which there appears to be no cause.

Q. What is the horse's natural reaction if frightened:
  (a) In the field?
  (b) In the stable?
  (c) When ridden?
A. (a) Runs away in a group and then stands at the end of the field looking back with head up and nostrils flared, maybe snorting.
A. (b) Head into the corner, bottom to the perceived danger.
A. (c) May buck, could rear; could try to run away from or spook at the perceived object of fear.

Q. What is likely to upset him?
A. Sudden noises or unexpected activity, particularly if he cannot see where the noise is coming from.

The Horse at Grass

Q. What is the normal behaviour in the field?

A. Horses grazing, usually in a group; some horses may be resting under a tree or just browsing in the sunshine. If cold and windy then horses tend to huddle together for communal shelter; they will turn their backs into the wind and weather. If content and secure then horses may lie down in the sun on a warm day.

Q. What sort of behaviour in the field would lead you to take a closer look at the horses?

A. One horse standing away from the group, either looking dejected or ostracised. One horse behaving differently or abnormally from the rest. All the horses running around looking anxious or harassed.

Q. What sort of behaviour can cause problems with groups of horses living together?

A. Sometimes geldings get possessive and fight each other if there is a mare in the group, particularly if she comes into season. If there is a dominant male horse he may threaten or bully other horses in the group causing them distress or anxiety. Generally, entire horses or rigs (horses which have not been completely or successfully castrated) should not be kept in the same field as geldings, and certainly not with mares.

Q. How would you expect a horse to behave when turned out after a long period of being stabled? When turning him out, why must you be careful?

A. He is likely to be highly excited, wanting to gallop about in the wide open space and then eventually to eat grass voraciously. When turning him out it would be wise to try to put him with a companion who is older and calm (and who has been out regularly) so that his desire to gallop is not encouraged by another horse behaving in the same way. Try to turn him out on a warm, sunny, quiet day when he is more likely to settle and eat, rather than a cold, windy day which is more likely to have him running about to keep warm. Try to turn him out when he is a bit hungry (just before a meal) so that he is more inclined to want to eat than to run.

Q. Some horses are difficult to catch. Why do you think this happens, and how can you use the horse's natural instincts to overcome this problem?

A. The horse may associate being caught with working and he may be reluctant to come in to work. He may enjoy his freedom and not wish to be stabled. He may want to stay with his friends, if you are trying to remove him from his companions. You can overcome this problem by catching all the other horses in the field first, so that the difficult-to-catch horse thinks he is going to be left on his own. Take the other horses to the gate as if to bring them out of the field. Tempt the difficult horse with food and then feed him when you bring him in, so that he associates coming in with food (before he has to work). Sometimes catch him, feed him and turn him out again, so that he does not always associate coming in with being worked.

Q. How might a horse, used to living out, behave in a strange field with a strange companion?

A. The horse may run around the perimeter of the field, literally examining the boundaries. He may sniff and squeal at his new companion; they may strike out at each other and then run around before hopefully settling to graze in close proximity to each other. If they do not settle, you may need to watch out for one horse harassing or bullying the other; in this case they may need to be separated.

Q. How might a horse behave if you separate him from his favourite companion by putting them in different fields?

A. He may be anxious and unsettled, running up and down the fence line or by the gate, calling to his friend. If the other horse is in earshot they may call to each other. In rarer circumstances one horse may try to jump out to rejoin his friend.

Q. How might a horse behave if you turn him out in a field on his own?

A. Some horses are used to going out alone and will be quite content. However, a horse used to company may be anxious; he will stay by the gate, pace up and down the fence, threaten to jump out and call and shout to anyone who may listen or answer him.

Q. You catch a horse and leave his companion alone in the field. How might the latter behave?

A. He may show signs of stressful behaviour and anxiety, as described in the preceding question.

Q. When releasing a horse into a field, what sort of behaviour might occur which would endanger you?

A. Turning horses out can be potentially dangerous for the handler. If a horse is excitable and anxious to get out to grass, he may try to dash off before you have completely released the headcollar. In this case you could receive a nasty wrench or pull on your fingers or arms. You should always turn the horse back towards the gate before letting him go, as then he must turn around before running away and this gives you a moment to move out of range. Horses often kick up their heels as they run off to play or eat, and it is very easy to receive a nasty kick from the heels of a disappearing horse.

Q. When releasing horses into a field, how might other horses behave if one horse is let go and gallops off?

A. If releasing more than one horse then there must be a signal between handlers to ensure that all horses are released at the same time. This minimises the risk of one horse charging off and the others trying to follow before the handlers are ready. If one horse is turned out into a field where other horses are already grazing, then the occupants may stop grazing and run up to the newcomer. They may then all run off together. As the handler, be ready to release the horse as quickly and efficiently as possible, and then stay out of the way of any approaching loose horses.

Q. It has been a cold, wet night. The horse is cold and miserable. How will it behave?

A. He will look dejected, head down, and huddled, perhaps against a hedge or fence line,trying to stay out of the wind. His coat will be wet and heavy, although if he has sufficient coat he should still be dry underneath the top, wet layer. He may be standing away from the rest of the group and will probably be keen to come in when you come to catch him. If very cold he may shiver visibly.

Q. Do horses lie down in the field? Is it a good sign when they do?

A. When horses are content and secure in their environment, and the weather is warm and sunny, then horses sometimes lie down. However, if a horse is lying down in inclement weather then this would not be a good sign.

The Horse in the Stable

Q. Why should you always speak to your horse before handling him?

A. So that the horse is aware of your presence and you do not take him by surprise, which might cause him to react instinctively (kick out or try to run away).

Q. Before touching a hind leg or foot, why should you pat the horse and run your hand along his body and down over his quarters?

A. The horse is then aware of where you are and which part of his body you are aiming for. If you touched a hind leg without any warning, the horse could react instinctively and kick out at you.

Q. What do the horse's ears tell you?

A. The ears indicate the horse's confidence and state of mind. If the horse is anxious his ears will be half turned back and look tense; if confident and happy, his ears will be forward and relaxed; if interested or alert, his ears will be pointed sharply forward. An angry or unhappy horse flattens his ears back against his head and looks miserable and bad-tempered.

Q. What do you have to be aware of when first working in the stable, or when grooming a strange horse?

A. The horse should always be tied up for his own and your safety. Be aware of the attitude of the horse: how confident he seems, how relaxed and happy he is – watch his body language and his ears. Move carefully and sympathetically around him at all times. Always let him know where you are and what you are about to do.

Q. A new horse comes into the yard. How might he behave if he has never been stabled before?

A. He may be anxious in the stable. He may rush to the door and look unsettled; he will not relax and be calm. Giving him a haynet may encourage him to settle and eat, as will putting him next door to another horse that he can see behaving in a calm, relaxed manner.

Q. If a horse is worried by new surroundings, what would be the signs?

A. The horse would look restless and unsettled. He may frequently pass small amounts of droppings. He may rush to the stable door, look out then pace around the stable. He won't settle and eat. His whole demeanour and body language is one of tension and anxiety.

Q. When you first handle a horse, what signs would tell you he was easy to handle?

A. He would be calm, relaxed and confident with you. His ears would be relaxed and happy; likewise his stance or movement in the stable would be relaxed. He would stand quietly while tied up, move over and pick up his feet with ease and without fuss. He would be quiet and enjoyable to work with.

Q. A horse is described as quiet to handle in the stable. How should he behave?

A. See the answer to the previous question. All these criteria apply.

Q. If a horse is inclined to bite, what precautions should you take before handling him or when adjusting his rugs?

A. Always tie up the horse before doing anything with him. If necessary, tie him quite short, or 'cross tie' him, i.e. attach a rope to each side of his headcollar so he cannot bite you from either side. Everyone involved in handling this horse should know about his bad habit, and only people competent in dealing with the fault should handle him.

Q. Do horses lie down in the stable? Is it a good sign if they do?

A. Some horses do lie down, particularly at night. The same criteria apply to the question of the horse lying down in the field. If the horse is secure and content he may lie down, and this demonstrates confidence. Unusual lying down, or lying down and showing signs of discomfort or pain, would cause concern.

The Horse when Ridden

Q. What sort of things affect a horse's behaviour when being ridden?

A. He may be upset by unfamiliar or sudden noises, particularly if he cannot see the source of the sound, e.g. a lawnmower. He may be frightened by black bin bags left out for the dustman. He may be less confident and more spooky if he is on his own. If riding outside in wind and rain he may be reluctant to 'face' into the bad weather.

Q. What type of horse do you consider suitable for a novice rider? How important is temperament?

A. A horse of some maturity and experience (not a very young, 'green' horse). A calm horse, and usually a half-bred horse or a 'cold-blooded' horse, not usually a thoroughbred. A horse with smooth, comfortable paces who reacts steadily and not suddenly or unpredictably. Temperament is very important. A calm, equable, amenable horse is ideal.

Q. We talk about horses having (a) a good temperament and (b) a nervous temperament. What do we mean?

A. (a) A good temperament is one where the horse is calm, predictable, pleasant to be around and to handle. He is tolerant of everything and nothing seems to bother him. He is biddable and amenable in every respect.

A. (b) A nervous temperament is one where the horse demonstrates anxiety and uncertainty in his behaviour. He is unpredictable and easily upset by the least change in circumstances. He is not calm or reliable.

Q. How would a horse show he was feeling fresh when he is first mounted?

A. He might not stand still and quietly while being mounted. He might become tight through his back and feel tense to the rider. He might try to rush off rather than wait for the rider's instruction. He might even try and put his head down and buck.

Q. What is a fresh horse?

A. A fresh horse is one who is feeling very full of himself. He may have been fed too much for the amount of work he is doing. He may have been shut in the stable and not turned out/worked hard for a day or two. He may just be feeling very well and on a bright spring day or a cold winter's day he just comes out feeling rather cheerful.

Q. How can you tell your horse is afraid of an object on the side of the road?

A. He will 'spook' at the object, trying to avoid going near it; he may try to run past it quickly because he is frightened of it. He may refuse to pass it, trying to turn around and go back the way he has come.

Q. How might your horse warn you that he is not happy about another horse approaching him in the ride?

A. He might lay his ears back and look angrily at the approaching horse. If the horse comes too close, he may turn his bottom towards it in a threatening gesture, or he may try to bite it. If it comes up behind him, your horse may stop abruptly and try to back up to the approaching horse and possibly kick out.

Q. What are the horse's natural defences when attacked?

A. To run away. To strike out at the danger with the hind feet, or, if necessary, with the front feet. To rear and swing around to avoid the attacker. If the 'attacker' is on his back then he would buck and plunge.

Taking the Exam

Examiners are professional instructors with many years' experience of training students and examining the standards they are aiming for. There will be a chief examiner, and probably two or three other examiners. They should all introduce themselves at the beginning of the day and they should wear a badge with their name on so that you can identify them. They are truly **human** and they like nothing better than to pass **everyone**. However, there is a standard to maintain and that is their responsibility. If you are up to standard **you will pass**. Examiners should smile and put you at your ease. They are **not** there to make the day traumatic for you; they are there to help you to do your best.

Exam psychology

You **must** go into the exam believing in yourself and in the competence you have achieved. If you have worked hard and have covered every aspect of the work required by the syllabus; if you can answer all the questions relative to the work at this level and can ride in a balanced co-ordinated way on sensible, trained horses; if you feel familiar with handling horses in the stable, carrying out the basic tasks required of this standard, then all you have to do on the day is go and show the examiners how competent you are.

Ultimately only you can dispel the nerves which inevitably will be there before you start. Do not allow nerves to fail you. You must learn to control them. Once you start the actual exam and have something to do, concentrate on the tasks and on showing your ability.

If you think you have made a mistake (and often you think that something is a major fault whereas the examiners think it a very minor fault!), put it behind you and think positively. Don't be so busy thinking about the error that you allow it to cloud the rest of the exam. Take the attitude that it will be the **only** fault you show, not the first of many. If you have trained hard enough then **you** (yes, **you**) have the capacity to pass. Go in and show the examiners how good you are.

Exam procedure

- The Stage 1 exam will take half a day. There will usually be up to eighteen candidates.

- You will be divided into three groups for the whole exam. Sometimes there are a few candidates taking just the riding section or the care section on its own. In this case they will join one of the groups for the section of the exam they are covering.

- The riding exam will usually take place in an indoor school, but in the summer, if the weather is good, it could be held on an outdoor surface. It will always be in a marked arena.

- You will ride two horses in the exam and this will give you the opportunity to demonstrate your competence equally on both horses. You may 'like' one horse better than the other, but do not allow this to inhibit you from riding competently at the level.

- On the first horse you will ride in your basic riding position, with stirrups at the length that you feel appropriate for work on the flat. At some time on the second horse you will be asked to take up your stirrups and demonstrate the jumping position in preparation for jumping.

- A member of staff from the riding centre will 'command' the ridden section. The caller/commander is there to help you do your best. If you need help or don't understand at any stage, then say so.

- The stable management testing will be covered in two or three sections.

- All the practical tasks will be carried out in the stable yard.

- You will work either individually with one horse per candidate or with another candidate sharing the same horse.

- If working alone, select the equipment you need and take it to the stable. If you need to leave the stable, for example to change something, always make sure that the horse is tied up and the stable door closed. Never leave the horse with equipment half on (e.g. don't leave the saddle on while going to fetch a girth!).

STAGE 1 – PROGRAMME

PROGRAMME A (maxiumum 18 candidates)

8.30   briefing

Element Nos	RIDE	PRACTICAL	PRACTICAL/ORAL
	1–12	1, 2, 3, 4	5, 6, 7, 8
	basic paces, on flat	grooming, clothing	horse husbandry
	& over poles	saddlery, handling	foot & shoeing
			anatomy & handling
			health & safety
09.00	Group A	Group C	Group B
10.00	Group B	Group A	Group C
11.00	Group C	Group B	Group A

12.00   **theory –** horse health, horse behaviour, basic grassland care, watering & feeding, general knowledge – elements 9, 10, 11, 12 and 13. *(Some elements may be examined in practical/oral section, if appropriate.)*

12.45   exam ends – lunch & summing up

If **theory** section (elements 9, 10, 11, 12 and 13) is divided into two or three groups at 12.00pm, each examiner should take parts of the syllabus and rotate to the two or three groups.

PROGRAMME B (maximum 18 candidates)

08.30   briefing

Element Nos	RIDE	PRACTICAL	PRACTICAL/ORAL
	1–12	1, 2, 3, 4	5, 6, 7, 8
	& then elements 9 & 13		& elements 10, 11, 12
	basic paces, on flat	saddlery, handling	horse husbandry
	& over poles	grooming, clothing	foot & shoeing
	horse health		anatomy & handling
	general knowledge		health & safety
			horse behaviour
			basic grassland care
			watering & feeding
09.00–10.15	Group A	Group B	Group C
10.15–11.30	Group B	Group C	Group A
11.30–12.45	Group C	Group A	Group B

12.45   exam ends – lunch & summing up

STAGE 1 PROG 2003

- If working with another candidate, always complete your own task so that you can talk about what you have done – for example, you put on the saddle, and the other person puts on the bridle.

- There will be a separate section where tasks such as standing the horse for inspection, mucking out, carrying weights, tying haynets, etc. are covered. This section will be attended by the whole group, with individuals being asked to carry out tasks while there is some communal discussion about the procedures.

- Make sure that you volunteer information whenever you can. Don't wait to be asked a question if there is an opportunity to show your knowledge without interrupting others.

- The examiner should control the group so that you all have the opportunity to input on each subject.

- The stable management theory section will cover all the subjects which are not covered by the practical work or which do not lend themselves to practical demonstration. These could include feeding, grassland and subjects such as the horse's behaviour when ridden and in the stable.

- The examiner should control the group, asking individuals to answer questions. Do take the opportunity to add information where you can, and if someone says something that you disagree with, be prepared to ask the examiner if you can add to what has been said and then politely state your opinion.

- Try to be clear and forthcoming in your discussion sections. Practise putting the information across in a clear, factual way which demonstrates your knowledge and does not waste time in 'waffle' without divulging any facts.

The next step and how to access it

If you are in a formal training situation (in a college or a training yard) you will probably receive plenty of guidance from your tutors or instructors as to how to proceed with your studies towards Stage 2. If you are working on BHS exams on your own, or perhaps receiving day-release training on a weekly or monthly basis, while working full-time in the horse industry, you may not be so clear as to how to progress towards Stage 2.

When you achieve any level of competence, then you must practise at that level, to consolidate the expertise, and not be in too much of a hurry to immediately aim for the next Stage. Have a long-term goal for achieving Stage 2 but allow yourself a little 'space' to enjoy your achievement at Stage 1 before loading yourself with further study. If you are working in the industry, then hopefully your practical day-to-day work will consolidate your competence and gradually you can study the requirements of the next level, beginning to plan how you will achieve the added expertise both in your riding and stable management skills.

Stage 2 will further challenge your riding ability and require that you are proficient in basic jumping. Stage 2 stable management will require that you are capable of looking after stabled horses or those kept at grass with a minimum of supervision for the basic, day-to-day requirements of those horses. The Stage exams are designed to allow you to progress smoothly from one level to another, ensuring that a thorough amount of hands-on practical experience is coupled with the theoretical knowledge.

Further Reading

The following books and booklets can all be obtained from the BHS Bookshop.

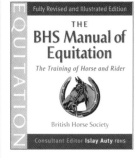

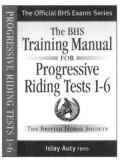

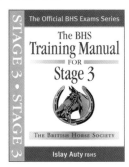

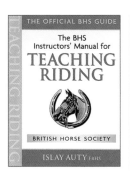
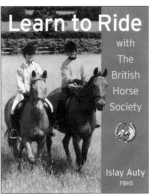
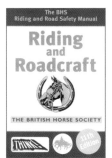
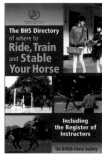

**Guide to BHS
Examinations**

**Examinations
Handbook**

**BHS Guide to Careers
with Horses**

Duty of Care

Useful Addresses

British Horse Society
Stoneleigh Deer Park
Kenilworth
Warwickshire
CV8 2XZ
tel: 08701 202244 or 01926 707700
fax: 01926 707800
website: www.bhs.org.uk
email: enquiry@bhs.org.uk

BHS Examinations Department
(address as above)
tel: 01926 707784
fax: 01926 707792
email: exams@bhs.org.uk

BHS Training Department
(address as above)
tel: 01926 707820
     01926 707799
email: training@bhs.org.uk

BHS Riding Schools/Approvals Department
(address as above)
tel: 01926 707795
fax: 01926 707796
email: Riding.Schools@bhs.org.uk

BHS Bookshop
(address as above)
tel: 08701 201918
     01926 707762
website: www.britishhorse.com

The BHS Examination System

Outline of progression route through
BHS examinations

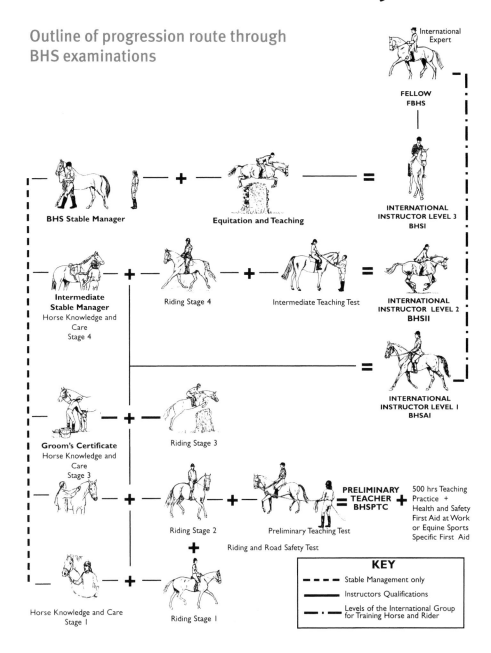

International
Expert

**FELLOW
FBHS**

**INTERNATIONAL
INSTRUCTOR LEVEL 3
BHSI**

BHS Stable Manager

Equitation and Teaching

**INTERNATIONAL
INSTRUCTOR LEVEL 2
BHSII**

**Intermediate
Stable Manager**
Horse Knowledge and
Care
Stage 4

Riding Stage 4

Intermediate Teaching Test

**INTERNATIONAL
INSTRUCTOR LEVEL I
BHSAI**

Groom's Certificate
Horse Knowledge and
Care
Stage 3

Riding Stage 3

**PRELIMINARY
TEACHER
BHSPTC**

500 hrs Teaching
Practice +
Health and Safety
First Aid at Work
or Equine Sports
Specific First Aid

Riding Stage 2

Preliminary Teaching Test

Riding and Road Safety Test

Horse Knowledge and Care
Stage 1

Riding Stage 1

KEY

- - - - Stable Management only

——— Instructors Qualifications

— · — Levels of the International Group
for Training Horse and Rider

notes

notes